Foreign Languages
in the
Elementary School

PRENTICE-HALL INTERNATIONAL, INC., London
PRENTICE-HALL OF AUSTRALIA, PTY., LTD., Sydney
PRENTICE-HALL OF CANADA, LTD., Toronto
PRENTICE-HALL FRANCE, S.A.R.L., Paris
PRENTICE-HALL OF INDIA (PRIVATE) LTD., New Delhi
PRENTICE-HALL OF JAPAN, INC., Tokyo
PRENTICE-HALL DE MEXICO, S.A., Mexico City

MARGUERITE ERIKSSON
York (Pa.) City Schools

ILSE FOREST
Western Reserve University

RUTH MULHAUSER
Western Reserve University

Foreign Languages
in the
Elementary School

PRENTICE-HALL, INC.
Englewood Cliffs, New Jersey

LB 1578
E68f

Foreword

This book does not purport to disclose any new points of view or the results of any new research on the subject of foreign languages in the elementary school. Rather it intends to synthesize the thinking of many people—specialists in foreign languages, educators, psychologists, anthropologists—whose combined thought has evolved a rapidly developing program in American education. The present text is intended for use in training elementary-school teachers of French. Much of the general discussion, such as on culture, audio-visual aids, and administration, is by no means limited to French. Some techniques of linguistic skills, however, are valid only in the framework of a specific language; for example, the problems in teaching French pronunciation are different from those involved in teaching Russian pronunciation to English-speaking children. Any discussion that attempts to generalize in this area will, by lacking in concreteness, inevitably be incomplete and inexact for a specific language. For this reason we have made an arbitrary choice of one language, but with no thought of suggesting any primacy in French over any other language with a written culture.

The choice of the two *programs* described is somewhat simpler: They are the programs best known to the authors. Stemming from two different philosophies and having different cultural and sociological environments, they complement each other well. Nevertheless, even with these major differences, there are definite points of agreement on techniques, teacher qualification, and administration. These are particularly noteworthy because of the other differences. We do not, however, mean to suggest these as the *only* alternatives, but merely as concrete examples of two successful programs.

The eclectic nature of this book creates in us a particular sense of gratitude to all those friends and colleagues who, directly or indirectly, in writing or by conversation, molded our thinking to the point of being able to write this text. Many an idea will not be credited to its originator simply because it cannot easily be traced back to a written source. Special mention is due, however, to Dr. Theodore Andersson of the University of Texas, Dr. Nelson Brooks of Yale University, Prof. Isabel M. Schevill of Stanford University, the Modern Language Association of America, and all those who took part in FLES Conferences 1955-1960. We should also like to add a special word of gratitude to Mr. Eugene K. Dawson, Supervisor of Foreign Languages in the Cleveland Public Schools, for his invaluable patience, aid, and understanding; to Dr. Victoria Lyles, former Supervisor of Elementary Education, who sparked the elementary French program in the York City Schools; and to Dr. John C. Albohm, former Superintendent of the York City Schools, under whose direction the York program reached its present stage of development. Dr. Mulhauser would like to express her deep appreciation to the American Association of University Women for their interest in another project that released time to aid with this book. Finally, we pay tribute to the vision of Dr. Emile B. de Sauzé, who headed a FLES Program in those lonely years before the Second World War. In the end, however, any shortcomings or inaccuracies in the book must be our responsibility.

Marguerite Eriksson
Ilse Forest
Ruth Mulhauser

Table of Contents

Foreign Languages

in the

Elementary School

Chapter I

FLES in Our Nation's Schools

FLES[1] expresses a new educational ideal that has been introduced into the curriculum of the American public school during the past two decades. There was precedent for teaching a second language in elementary grades when in 1952 Dr. Earl J. McGrath, then U. S. Commissioner of Education delivered to the Central States Modern Language Association what was to become an historic address in which he urgently advocated the study of a foreign language in elementary school. French had been taught in the schools of Cleveland as a way of enriching the curriculum for gifted children for thirty years; P.S. 208 Brooklyn, a school for talented pupils in the Greater New York System, had included foreign languages in its elementary curriculum since the nineteen thirties; there were still other significant experiments underway conducted principally by members of college and university language departments and enrolling mostly "volun-

---

[1] *FLES* is the accepted abbreviation for "Foreign Languages in the Elementary School."

teer" pupils. In addition, the years following World War II had provided a general climate favorable toward the study of other languages in the interest of promoting intercultural understanding. The way had therefore been paved for the more firmly established experiments that followed Dr. McGrath's exhortation.

At present many communities throughout the United States are providing FLES courses, and there is a growing trend toward including in such courses many pupils who are not classified as "gifted" but who are nevertheless judged capable of carrying a second language as a means of enriching their elementary school education. Yet the future of FLES is still undecided. The countrywide adoption of the plan must wait not merely upon the decision of school administrators or even school boards but upon the will of the American public. The public at large will require not merely pedagogical justification of a second language at the elementary level but also the sociological and psychological reasons for including FLES as an integral part of the curricula of tax-supported elementary schools throughout the nation.

FLES AND THE ELEMENTARY SCHOOL CURRICULUM

During the last six years the work of our public schools has been subjected to continuous reappraisal both from within the group of professional educators responsible for their administration and conduct and from the lay citizenry. Among the latter are included representatives of government, industry, the armed services, the church, and the tax-paying public at large. There had been criticism aplenty even before the launching of Sputnik and the realization that something must be done were we to compete with Russia's dramatic successes in scientific fields. Paul Woodring's book, *A Fourth of a Nation*, appearing almost simultaneously with Russia's man-made satellite, reflected the views of a large segment of our educational leadership and at the same time appealed strongly to thoughtful lay critics of our schools and of the progressive era in American education generally believed to be responsible for Ivan's triumph over Johnny in scholastic honors. Muted expressions of discontent changed to loud demands for a change of policy that would encourage gifted boys and girls especially to work to their fullest capacity rather than permitting them to saunter along at the pace of the less talented majority. From the professional group by way of rejoinder came the demand for better trained teachers, better school buildings, superior modern equipment, a specialized nonteaching staff to supplement the work of the instructional staff. These changes entailed higher budgets and the levies which must accompany them.

The pressures upon school personnel from a tax-paying public demanding full production through more efficient administration and better teaching have steadily increased. Young teachers of a generation ago were indoctrinated with the idea of gently "leading" their pupils; now the beginner is exhorted to drive youngsters into and through the green pastures of learning as rapidly as efficiency permits. "Frills" in the curriculum are discouraged in favor of fundamentals. Consequently those who believe in the value of FLES must be prepared to defend it by convincing the public that teaching a foreign language to elementary pupils over a period of years—years representing two or more in the elementary grades and a continuing span of time in the junior high school—by a direct method, will result in the acquisition of a second language coordinate with the mother tongue. They must also seek support by showing ways in which this second tongue may be of value not merely as "enrichment" but in its own right as a means of deepening young America's understanding of cultural differences as well as cultural similarities among the peoples of the earth. School officers as well as the public will need reassurance as to whether or not the addition of a foreign language will fragment yet further a curriculum believed by many to be overly segmented already. Should a foreign language be added to a curriculum that already includes music, art, physical education, field trips, and school camping?

Actually, a foreign language lends itself beautifully to integration where there is good professional cooperation between classroom teachers and FLES instructors. Literature, art, and social studies may be greatly enriched through association with a specific culture that is gradually becoming familiar to pupils through their study of the culture's language.

Surely there is no greater need at present than communication and improved understanding among peoples, and few will deny that knowing a second language intimately helps in understanding "the other" and "the foreign."

FLES AND THE ELEMENTARY SCHOOL PUPIL

Modern educational theory emphasizes the necessity for active involvement and high interest on the part of pupils in successful learning activity. Many children are excited and eager about learning a foreign language; others may be indifferent or even resentful of any addition to their school program. The FLES teacher confronts accordingly a problem of motivation, of stimulating interest where it is lacking and then maintaining it at a high level. To be successful in his task the teacher needs to know something about the personal qualities and educational status of the pupils with whom he is dealing; they on their part must understand his aims and also what is expected of them during the FLES period.

The elementary school pupil is well adapted to the learning of a foreign language by the direct method. In the majority of cases he is quite flexible and able to imitate the pronunciation of the teacher with remarkable fidelity. As one authority comments: ". . . the elementary school age has been advocated as the best period for language learning because the child is less self-conscious. He is more willing to make strange sounds and to take part in activities which the self-conscious adolescent will shun for fear of being laughed at." [2] As the youngster progresses through the grades, he grows not only in intellectual maturity but also in the direction of getting down to work promptly and efficiently. He improves markedly in his command of his native language. In the third grade he is in process of becoming an independent reader through increasing his skills in using phonics and other cues for word attack and for deriving meanings. He is able to use his reading skill in perusing easy supplementary material as well as his basic text. His relative maturity in comparison with the first or second grader, especially in his command of his native language makes the third grade pupil appear to be just the right young person to start a new language. There is little risk that his adventures with foreign language patterns will interfere with his progress in the mother tongue. The possibility that there might be such interference

---

[2] Harold B. Dunkel, *Second-Language Learning* (Boston: Ginn & Company, 1949), p. 72.

in the case of school beginners deters many teachers from advocating a kindergarten, first grade, or even second grade starting point. The third grader is interested in investigating his native environment, and his social studies course may take him farther afield by means of stories, film strips, and other media. He is probably widening his acquaintance with distant places by watching TV. A skillful teacher should have little difficulty in interesting him in the activity of pattern practice.

The fourth grade pupil is further along in independent reading than he was last year; his curiosity is lively and he is eager for novel experiences. He delights in physical activity and tasks requiring long periods of sitting still must be interesting indeed to hold his attention. Typically he enjoys his science work and likes to do independent research, reporting his findings to the class. If he has been well taught, he enjoys the newer arithmetic program and takes pride in handing in good papers. He likes to participate in classroom activities such as elections, decision-making discussions, and consideration of possible class projects. He loves variety and will throw himself into any interesting group undertaking, carrying his responsibilities for various activities with credit and success provided he does not need to work at them continuously for too long a period of time. Actually he has reached what some psychologists call "the maturity of childhood" and is thoroughly enjoying himself with few problems related to his growth to trouble him. He loves games and plays vigorously although in a more headlong, undisciplined fashion than he will a year or two hence. A lively, cheerful teacher may expect to accomplish much with him, either in FLES or any other curriculum area. The key is to capture his interest and enthusiasms, keep him moving mentally and physically, and make sure he derives well-earned pleasure from the end products of his labors.

Fourth grade pupils like to communicate and do so quite effectively; fifth and sixth graders have developed even greater facilities in the language arts and typically love to employ these in sharing their thoughts, dreams, and convictions with others. Fourth graders are usually slow and laborious writers; the upper elementary pupil writes quite easily and fluently when he has something to say or when the task assigned is not too long. Many of these older children read widely for pleasure and, when they are encouraged at home, take a keen interest in current events. Their personal reading

interests include nonfiction as well as fiction; many of them read
books about vocations because they are beginning to think realistically
about the future. Their horizons are broadening, partly because
their social studies curriculum carries them to other lands; they
study about life in Mexico and South America as well as the United
States and are beginning to understand something about their
country's relation to the family of nations.

It is most important that the FLES teacher recognize and
challenge this growing maturity by adapting FL teaching to the
rapidly expanding interests of these older pupils.

Nevertheless these are still children with short attention spans
in comparison with the attention spans of adults. They cannot be
expected to sit still, concentrate, and respond to questions for long
periods of time. They are usually interested in learning French, but
they do not have the driving urge to learn possessed by most adults,
for instance, who are studying a foreign language for vocational
interests or for travel. The successful FLES teacher will learn to
hold their attention and heighten their interest by varying his
activities in accordance with their other preferred pursuits; for
instance, they love to dance and sing and work on projects and listen
to stories about how other people live. These concerns may be used
by the FLES teacher both to his own advantage and to that of the
classroom teacher.

MOTIVATING THE FLES PUPIL

Creating real motivation is one of the very difficult tasks required
of the teacher. Although the inexperienced sometimes think motivation to be just a matter of "getting them interested" at the beginning
of a lesson, what is really needed is a performance more like lighting
a spark that will in turn arouse a response in the youngsters' minds
leading to sustained activity in the direction desired by the teacher.
As one authority puts it: "Motivation is activity by one person
designed to stimulate or arouse a state within a second person or
group that under appropriate circumstances initiates or regulates
activity in relation to goals."[3] As the same author indicates, the term

---

[3] Herbert J. Klausmeier, *Learning and Human Abilities: Educational Psychology*
(New York: Harper & Row, Publishers, 1961), p. 320.

motivation also refers to the state within the learner which rises as a result of this (teacher) activity. In the second sense "motivation" has a certain intensity—high, low, or average.

In almost every school population one may count upon a sizeable group of youngsters who are highly motivated with respect to school tasks generally and are eager to learn almost any new subject. To these the learning of a second language represents a delightful opportunity to show what they can do with a novel challenge and to enjoy the triumph accompanying success. Such pupils typically set their own high goals for each FLES period and pursue these with a will. These students respond with enthusiasm to discussions of what a second language may contribute to an individual's success in life, socially and in business; they see the advantages of understanding another culture better through knowing the language of the people; of extending the range of their communication skills and, as a result, their acquaintance with literature. However, in many cases there will be also enrolled in the FLES program another group who have little interest in academic achievement generally and little or no incentive to study a foreign language. In dealing with these pupils the teacher should make serious effort to find out what orientations they do in fact possess and toward what constructive goals they may be directed easily. Self-esteem and self-actualization are two universal human needs. The FLES teacher should find ways to relate the second language to the ambitions of the nonacademic pupil whose need for self-actualization does not include success in academic pursuits. For these boys and girls the social assets of knowing a second language may well have some appeal, as may the advantages in conducting a business or perhaps in securing a certain kind of job. These possibilities should be indicated and developed through discussion, and wherever possible they should be illustrated.

Among the group of the disinclined there may be a number whose objections to attempting something new are based on the experience of failure in connection with the regular school curriculum. It is most important that the FLES instructor arouse the interest of these pupils and encourage them to make even the smallest response which can be rewarded with praise for success.

The following pupil comments, representing the FLES students of one small American city, give some indication of what youngsters throughout the country might think and are suggestive of some approaches which may ignite the spark of motivation.

I like French very much, and I think it has helped me to become better acquainted with the country of France. I liked studying about food best of all. If I do take French in junior high, I am sure that two years of French that I have had will help me very much.

I liked French this year very much. The language is not too hard and not too easy. I like the system by which it is being taught. The teachers are good and the materials are nice. I plan to continue this language in my junior and senior high school years.

I have enjoyed learning French. We have done many interesting things in our French class. Some day I would like to be able to speak French well enough to talk to a French person and have a nice conversation.

This year I enjoyed French very much. I have learned many new and interesting facts about the French people, their homes, and their daily lives.

I think whether you like French or not depends on you and your teacher, and I think I have had two of the best teachers. I have a pen pal. I wrote three times and got back three. I haven't gotten a letter for three months.

I am going to take a sewing course this summer. They have prizes for the winners of the best dress you make and one of the prizes is a trip to Paris. I would like to climb up the Eiffel Tower some day. . . . My little sister and I sometimes like to play French class, and I try to teach her something, but she doesn't understand it too well.

Negative comments, too, are not without interest for the would be motivator.

It—French—interferes with other school work. Sometimes when we were taking a test the French teacher would come in and we would have to put everything away.

I don't like French because I think it is hard to speak, but it is still a good language.

It is tiresome sitting in the class when having French. I hate to write in the French notebook putting in all those accents and writing.

Evidently these youngsters had assessed the value of a second language realistically. On the positive side, they appreciate learning about a foreign culture, such as about French food, the daily lives of French people, their homes. One pupil appreciates the "system," that is, the direct method, by which he had been taught. Another thinks she had fine teachers. Still another has ambitions for climbing the famous Eiffel Tower and tries to teach her little sister French. One commentator *doesn't* like French because it interferes with the regular schedule, another finds it hard to speak—but a *good* language. Finally, in this random sample, there is one who doesn't like writing—especially not when there are "accents." The wise FLES teacher will plan accordingly by enthusiastically setting forth the good things in store for the future—like travel and meeting French people—and by keeping at a minimum the things about learning a language which will always seem tiresome to certain boys and girls.

FLES AND THE CLASSROOM TEACHER

A good rapport between the classroom teacher and the FLES instructor is of basic importance in the development of a successful foreign-language program. Such a relationship is readily established when each teacher is determined to strengthen the other's efforts in every way possible. From the FLES standpoint correlation between the foreign-language study and the school's regular social science program has been noted as highly desirable. Similarly, when the classroom teacher is wise enough to use the language instructor's understanding of a foreign culture by involving the visitor in curriculum planning, the pupils' social studies experiences may be greatly enriched.

The classroom teacher can help the visiting teacher in various ways. Perhaps he can offer good suggestions as to methods of teaching the particular class the two are sharing. Often he can help by interpreting to the visitor the special needs of individual pupils. Such combined effort accomplishes much toward the effective integration of FLES with the curriculum of the American elementary school.

Chapter II

Preliminary Considerations

Fundamentally the linguistic skills which we want to develop in our elementary school children are these: we want to give them a complete control of the sound system, and we want to teach them to use the second language as normal speech. All phases of foreign-language teaching should lead directly or indirectly to the achievement of these goals. We teach the children to express complete ideas using basic speech patterns. Language learning is cumulative. We who are privileged to begin teaching foreign language to pupils of elementary school age must lay a foundation that is just as solid as one started in secondary school, although it is accomplished by different means. Our teaching is limited to hearing and speaking for a much longer time, and the methods of presentation must conform to the age and interests of younger children, but all language teachers' aims are fundamentally identical. We are consciously equipping our pupils with basic constructions and vocabulary that are essential in any subsequent work. FLES should never be considered a "prelude to 'real' language learning (which will begin in the high school) rather than a serious, systematic attempt to develop attitudes and skills."[1]

Even before the teacher ever puts a foot into the classroom, he must have certain policies, principles, and techniques clearly in mind; for a great proportion of his teaching is sheer habit formation, and deviations from a single pattern will only nullify that habit formation process and produce confusion in its wake. Language habits will be formed in the children gayly and unconsciously as long as they feel secure and relaxed, rewarded for their effort by a sense of power that comes from communication. For some time, this power of communication is entirely dependent on the teacher's thorough understanding and acceptance of precision in habit formation as the means to communication. Discourse patterns, the forms of address, and the use of the new language in the classroom are several points which must be thoroughly regulated and admit of no deviation from the very first day of school. In addition, the basic philosophy of the program will have influenced the course of study and the planned continuity of the language learning experience.

DISCOURSE PATTERNS

Linguistic science has made eminently clear that communication is based on patterns, that is, words in a meaningful context. One of the easiest and most euphoria producing traps in FLES teaching is vocabulary teaching, particularly of nouns. Countless objects are enumerated correctly in the foreign language and the child seems to have a wide linguistic knowledge when, in fact, he knows only one pattern of sentence. (*C'est un livre, une chaise, une table*, etc.) It is our firm conviction that the teacher's guiding principle from the very beginning must be that structural patterns should be taught rather than isolated words. The sentence is the unit of importance. It is equally important for the teacher to remain aware of the interchangeability of words within a pattern. "Undue emphasis on words as words to the neglect of pronunciation and grammatical structure is

[1] "A Survey of FLES Practices," Nancy V. Alkonis and Mary A. Brophy, *Reports of Surveys and Surveys of Studies in the Teaching of Modern Foreign Language Association* (Washington, D.C.: U. S. Government Printing Office, 1961), p. 217.

not in keeping with modern linguistic thinking. . . . On the other hand, one cannot deny or ignore the existence of the word as a tangible unit of language." [2] Words learned in patterns are more easily and permanently retained, and patterns give a kind of semantic emphasis to key words. It has been further established that pupils remember nouns easily when associated with objects or pictures and they remember verbs which are associated with actions. They like to deal with tangible things even at the age of ten years and it is best not to neglect this natural motivation but to channel it into good linguistic pattern learnings.

THE USE OF ENGLISH

The second principle which must be thoroughly explored and defined quite rigidly before the first day of school is that of the use of the foreign language in the classroom. In some school systems the foreign-language teachers have adopted the "no English" rule. They have found that by skillful manipulating of the language, it is possible to develop a degree of comprehension on the part of the pupils which makes it unnecessary to resort to English. In such a situation the use of English is not permitted; the teacher leads the class by the inductive process from one thought to another until a logical conclusion is reached. If the class does not understand at first, the teacher may continue talking around the subject, using familiar vocabulary until some pupil "catches on"; or by a series of related questions directed to one or more pupils, he may lead them to a final understanding of the original question and help them formulate the answer. The teacher may then continue with similar questioning, thus giving the class the opportunity of hearing the same construction several times, using a different noun or making whatever substitution is possible within the structure pattern. No explanation has been given in English, yet the teacher has made sure that everyone in the class understands. This method is often found in programs where the foreign language is taught every day to selected pupils of above average ability, though it need by no means be confined to such a group.

---

[2] Robert Lado, *Linguistics Across Cultures* (Ann Arbor, Mich.: University of Michigan Press, 1957), p. 75.

However, the teacher must use great skill to lead a class inductively and efficiently to the right conclusion.

In other school systems, however, English is permitted at certain specific moments such as when introducing a new song, in taking disciplinary action, or in setting the stage for a dialogue that takes place in an imaginary situation such as asking directions or buying a gift in a foreign store. Even in the early years the use of English may also be allowed for the inclusion of some cultural material. "Understanding between peoples does not automatically result from language study. It must be included as a definite teaching objective." [3] Even in pure language drill, although translation is unwise most of the time, there are some occasions when it may seem best in order to avoid confusing the pupils and impeding further progress in the use of the pattern or expression involved. Most of the time, however, the foreign-language teacher will set up a stimulus-response situation by the question-answer technique or pattern practice until through constant repetition the response becomes automatic. As a teacher gains more experience, he tends to use less English in the classroom. Those who want to permit the judicious use of English must formulate a few simple but absolute rules to guide themselves through difficult situations and avoid wasting time. Every word of English spoken during the foreign-language period is in one sense at least one bit of time stolen from foreign-language training. It must be justifiable on some very specific ground related to the central philosophy of the program.

> A skilled teacher may successfully conduct every lesson entirely in the second language, and up to the point of diminishing returns, French should be the exclusive medium. If the second language is presented throughout as an entity in itself, and never as an equivalent of English the latter may be used sparingly without harm when necessity requires. But if English is spoken more than incidentally, watch out! [4]

Whatever the "ground rules" are to be, they must be decided before the first class. The teacher must accept them totally and by example

---

[3] J. C. Albohm, "Foreword," *First Year Course of Study for the Teaching of French in the Elementary School*, rev. ed. (York, Pa.: York School District, 1960), p. i.

[4] Nelson Brooks, et al., *Beginning French in Grade Three* (New York: Modern Language Association of America, 1955), p. vii.

make them clear and acceptable to the pupils, for foreign-language learning is truly a skill subject in which one learns by doing.

TERMS OF ADDRESS

The question of the terms of address taught to and used with children has both philosophic and practical aspects. Philosophically, the *tu* form is used in the classroom situation in France by most teachers until the age of eleven or even later. Adults habitually use this form when speaking to children to say nothing of the many other situations in which the familiar form is used. These general situational rules may be formulated and explained quite simply in English at the beginning of school. The explanation need be no more complicated than the following:

> There are two ways to say "you" in French: *tu* and *vous*. This is the way we will use them: *tu* will be used in the following situations:
>
> 1. when the teacher speaks to one pupil
> 2. when one pupil speaks to another
> 3. when the class speaks to one pupil
>
> *vous* will be used in the following situations:
>
> 1. when one pupil speaks to the teacher
> 2. when anyone speaks to the class or more than one person
> 3. when the speakers do not know each other very well

The children very quickly become familiar with the correct use of *tu* and *vous* if the teacher is careful to plan the situations with this new pattern in mind until it has become automatic.

In systems where the *tu* form is taught, the change from *tu* to *vous* between the pupils themselves is usually made in the seventh grade.

> In the secondary school the emotional climate of the classroom is quite different, and the "tu" form is frequently no longer appropriate. This would seem to be the logical time to introduce the polite form. The child who learns in this manner is following the same sequence of development as the French child, emotionally, socially and linguistically. . . . The important thing is that he complete the learning cycle with a clear idea of the relationship which exists between feeling and form, and not just a theoretical knowledge about children, servants and pets, but a real knowledge, which he has lived.
>
> These reasons lead me to believe there is an advantage in using the familiar form in the primary school classroom. The results may not

be visible for a while, but I feel that in the long run, such a pattern of learning will produce young people who are capable of sharing with their French neighbors a new and different way of thinking about human relationships. And after all, is that not one of our foremost reasons for teaching them French in the first place?[5]

Some very experienced FLES teachers prefer, however, to teach only the *vous* form to the children from the very beginning. These teachers maintain that it is the general form of address and should be completely automatic to any nonnative speaker of French. They also maintain that it is less confusing to the child in the early stages of learning and that the familiar form may be easily learned later in a situation where it is needed and appropriate. The partisans of the *tu* form think it best to accustom the children to its use because it is an inherent part of the language and the children will not be surprised by it in their later study. Furthermore, they will already have had drill to the point where they can use both forms interchangeably.

The practical aspect of the question is slightly different. The linguistic skill required of the teacher himself is immeasurably greater when he undertakes to teach, drill, and have used in free conversation both forms of address, rather than just the polite *vous* form. It must be assumed, therefore, that the teachers in the program are sufficiently fluent in French to use both forms without impairing their efficiency as language teachers. It is our opinion that even though the exclusive use of *vous* from the third grade through the twelfth simplifies greatly the problem of teaching, the linguistic and cultural rewards accrued to the children through learning to handle both forms accurately and automatically far outweigh the complications involved in the teaching situation *if the teacher can handle both forms easily himself.* This is certainly one of the points where any program attempting to use incompletely trained teachers should choose to follow the simpler method rather than to fall short by attempting too much.

COURSE OF STUDY

The decisions made on the foregoing points will greatly influence the choice of a course of study to be used by the teachers during the elementary school years. Just after World War II, it was quite normal for each FLES teacher to create his own course of study. This

---

[5] Robert Brooks, "Problèmes de français à l'école américaine—'tu' ou 'vous'?" *Cités unies*, No. 7 (April, 1958), 41.

practice had the merit of producing material completely adapted to the particular circumstances in which the teacher or group of teachers were working. Since then, however, much progress has been made. The Modern Language Association of America devoted much time, labor, and the specialized knowledge of authorities in the fields of linguistics, child psychology, foreign-language teaching, elementary education and cultural anthropology to create materials for the teaching of several languages at the elementary level. These materials have become models for most organized courses of study written in the past ten years. Experience has shown that the new teacher now would be extremely unwise to undertake to write his own course of study, for such a venture requires an inordinate amount of time as well as highly specialized technical knowledge to guarantee the optimum results.

It is equally true, nevertheless, that the FLES program which succeeds best is the one which is most carefully integrated into the overall educational aims of a particular school system. A district that decides on a program for all children, emphasizing the cultural aspects equally with the linguistic, obviously cannot expect to attain the same level of linguistic skill for the children as another program which either does not emphasize the culture or is given to only a selected segment of the group. Such a decision need not, however, greatly influence the choice of a course of study if the course is scientifically planned. Rather it will determine the actual daily planning and the extent of use of the manual. The wisest FLES teachers of long experience have never stopped repeating that at the elementary level, quantity has relatively no importance: quality is the key word. A little language, well taught and learned, is the firm foundation on which all future language learning depends.

The course of study, then, will be chosen carefully among the many good ones whose value has been proved by successful use in the classroom. Once chosen, this course of study will most probably need to be adapted to the particular program in which it is to be used. Five simple questions may provide answers of great value in choosing such a manual:

1. Is there a real and gradual progression in structural patterns?
2. Is there evidence of planned re-entry of patterns and vocabulary?
3. Is the material presented situationally?

4. Are the subjects presented compatible with the plan of this program for correlation and experience?
5. Does the manual lend itself to adaptation? For example, can it be cut without losing its validity for interest or language learning?

Once the course of study or teacher's manual is chosen, the central policy for the program has been set. There still remains, however, the important, meticulous, and creative work of adapting this material to the particular system and then to the individual classes within the overall philosophy expressed in the choice of manual.

CONTINUITY OF THE PROGRAM

In many ways, the most important policy decision to which there must be thorough commitment is the overall philosophy underlying all foreign-language teaching in the elementary schools and more particularly in the individual school system. In a country as vast as the United States with a tradition of local self-determination in the education of its children, it would hardly be reasonable to expect to find a uniform policy on a particular subject matter. We have already seen several possible choices of some importance both in choosing which children will receive instruction in foreign language and in choosing the kind of instruction they will receive. We have also considered the nature of language learning emphasizing its cumulative habit-formation characteristics. In short, the linguistic nature of such instruction inevitably requires a clear policy on the continuation of foreign-language learning. In this particular matter, moreover, even no policy at all is a policy; namely, a commitment to exposure to foreign-language learning for a period of time with no thought of bringing it to a high-level skill.

Authorities are now unanimous in the opinion that the best and most efficient FLES program is only the first step in an unbroken language sequence through the twelfth grade. There is no implication that such continuity must be rigid or compulsory but only that the FLES program best fulfills its potential when any individual child who shows aptitude and interest can continue to build on the foundation he has received in the elementary school. The practical implications of such a policy will be discussed more fully in Chapter IX, but the commitment and policy must be clear before the teacher begins his first class.

Chapter III

Pronunciation, Presentation, Drill & Scenes

PRONUNCIATION

The determination to work for good pronunciation habits without sacrificing fluency should be established before the foreign-language teacher starts a program, should be maintained throughout the year, and should be reaffirmed at the beginning of each succeeding year when it is usually necessary to revive good habits lost during vacation. In the first lesson much drill is needed on these simple words: *Bonjour, Mademoiselle, Madame, Monsieur.* The pupils tend to miss the nasal sound, substitute "ma-dam" for "mad-moi" ("mwa") and produce an American "l" or "r." The name *Marianne* can easily become Mary Ann unless the teacher exercises great care and refuses to accept an anglicized pronunciation. Unless the teacher makes a patient, consistent effort to help the pupils develop a *new set of pronunciation* habits in the beginning lessons, the new language will be spoken with the customary lack of lip movement noticeable in everyday American speech. The teacher must emphasize these lip movements and the rigidity of the position; he must teach the children to hear the differences between the sounds in the two languages, for this is the first step in training aural comprehension. The hearer doesn't always hear exactly what is said; he tends to hear what he thinks he hears. It is a familiar fact of psychology that perception through any sense organ is affected by the interpretation being given to that perception.

A large percentage of children can imitate correct French pronunciation with ease, but it is a task of considerable magnitude to succeed in establishing this correctly imitated pronunciation as a firm habit. Robert Lado, in the foreword to *Linguistics Across Cultures*, discusses cogently the special problems arising from any effort to develop a new set of language habits. Through a presentation of the foreign language in direct comparison with the vernacular equivalent one may pinpoint the problems encountered by the pupils in connection with pronouncing the foreign words. Here are some of these difficulties and some techniques suggested to overcome them.

Pupils do not move their lips enough and therefore produce indistinct and distorted sounds. From the very first day the teacher should make clear to the children that they are expected to imitate his pronunciation and that it is produced by certain movements of the lips and tongue that differ from English. He should emphasize that French or the foreign language in question is made up of a whole system of sounds different from the sounds in English words.

Simple drills on sound placement may well be treated as games. They serve as pronunciation practice and relaxation from other activities. One extremely simple drill-game can be played by having the pupils make the following sounds: a consonant and a vowel pronounced clearly and distinctly forward in the mouth with precise differences between the vowels: "pa," "pe," "pi," "po," "pu," "ba," "be," "bi," "bo," "bu," "va," "ve," "vi," "vo," "vu," etc. The consonants may be chosen either for their close but different positions or their widely differing positions. Short meaningful sentences repeating the same vowel sound or contrasting two confused sounds may also be used. Analysis of sound and phonetic theory is of relatively little value with young children and hence not recommended.

Simple trial and error with ample praise received for precise success normally proves more effective. A mirror is often helpful in enabling a child to see the position of his lips when making a new sound. Teaching by rough equivalents in English sounds is a questionable practice, for the child may well produce only the English sound that is *not* a precise equivalent. Furthermore, such equivalents are usually based on standard American pronunciation with no consideration of regional differences; hence the equivalent may be totally inaccurate for the particular group. In large industrial cities, moreover, the speech of all the individual children in a class will probably not be identical. The wisest path, therefore, proves to be that of taking time and care to develop precise articulation.

All errors in pronunciation are, in the last analysis, faulty articulation; but what is meant here is insufficient or slow and imprecise movement of the lips and tongue. A simple exercise or game in "silent lip reading" where the teacher leads the class in a choral repetition but utters no sound may help to form the habit of moving the lips and tongue precisely. Exaggerated movement should be encouraged in the first stages, for normal human economy of movement will bring the exaggeration back into line. Children also enjoy repeating lists of words containing the same sound. Such lists, especially when the sound (like *soeur*) is not found in English have the effect of magic incantations dear to children even as they provide practice in the new muscular coordination involved in making the sound and in moving to it from various other sound positions.

A second result of faulty articulation is the quite natural one of substituting English articulation for closely related sounds in the foreign language. In this area the teacher must assure himself first that the sound has been heard correctly. Many students substitute a familiar English sound for an unrecognized French one; thus *bleu* becomes "blur" or "blue," *huit* becomes "wheat" and *quinze* becomes "cans." The sound "oo" is substituted for the French "u" in *tu*, and the English word "crayon" is often substituted for *le crayon* by beginning pupils. "We have ample evidence that when learning a foreign language we tend to transfer our entire native language system in the process."[1]

Frequently the simplest way is to contrast the English and French sounds asking the children *Est-ce le même?* or *Répète le son français.* Once assured that the sound has been *heard* correctly, the teacher will find correcting the child's articulation much simpler. When the

---

[1] Robert Lado, *Linguistics Across Cultures* (Ann Arbor, Mich.: University of Michigan Press, 1957), p. 11.

right sound has been obtained, it must be drilled both in series and in contrast.

Children, indeed most nonnative speakers, tend to blur very common sounds of structural importance. Since French gender is grammatical, a new concept to Anglo-Saxons, and of no philosophic value to the child, it is extremely important that he unconsciously but precisely attach the correct article to each word. Much contrastive drill on the differences between *le, la* and *les* as well as *un* and *une* will be required, but the end rewards are invaluable. Momentary inattention may also result in aural confusion of closely related words like *vert, verte; mon, ton, son,* etc. Such errors call for immediate correction to avoid bad habit formation, but they are not essentially problems of pronunciation.

Precision in the individual sounds is only the beginning of good pronunciation, for just as the sentence or pattern is the basis of language structure rather than the individual word, so the sentence or utterance is the basic unit of which the individual sound is only a part. In all connected speech, some sounds are swallowed and there is a definite tone pattern significant to any native speaker. The French tone pattern parallels that of English at certain points, for example, rising inflection on questions; but on the whole, it is distinctive and different. The lack of individual word accent but the presence of sentence accent is perhaps the most striking difference. Naturally, of course, the teacher is the first and basic model for the children. It cannot be overstressed, therefore, *that the teacher's own pronunciation must be impeccable:* the model must be worthy of imitation by all the youngsters who will copy it both unconsciously and consciously. There are, nevertheless, a certain number of natural errors which will appear because of the children's already set habits in English. Cognate words present special difficulty in that they will be accented as in English. Sentences with emotional stress (joy, sorrow, etc.) particularly when they are completely understood, will be expressed in Anglo-Saxon emotional inflection. Here again, contrasting repetition will help the children's linguistic habits and incidentally teach an excellent lesson in cultural differences.

The sentence pattern should also be emphasized as normal speech at a normal rate of speech. Authorities differ on the advisability of breaking the sentence down further into sound groups. Some people believe this practice creates only overprecise, artificial and an abnormally slow production of speech. We are convinced, however, that the individual sounds must be precise (including the precise slurring of *J'm'lève*) but that automaticity can be judged complete only when the child attains something approximate to native speed and intonation of utterance.

One brief concluding remark is necessary about the teaching of pronunciation. It is the Scylla and Charybdis of every language teacher, new or experienced. Sensitivity to the frustration threshold of a particular class or an individual pupil is of prime importance. Adequate drill in correct pronunciation must counterbalance uncorrected and inaccurate sounds accepted at certain moments to permit fluent self-expression. Special drills on contrasting sounds in the two languages may help accuracy and ease of sound production. In the end, however, the pupil must arrive somewhere between being completely inhibited in spite of a "perfect accent" and being extremely fluent in an unrecognizable French. The problem of pronunciation is omnipresent, vital but soluble.

TECHNIQUES OF PRESENTATION AND DRILL

It seems fitting to discuss at some length the various techniques employed in teaching our pupils to use the second language as normal speech. Choral response, pattern practice, "conversation," and dialogues and scenes are all important techniques for developing normal speech in the second language. Sympathy and imaginative consideration for the muscular fumblings of the neophyte speakers, as well as a constant personal reminder that the behavior of the learner is the focal point for the technique used, will help to maintain a fluid adaptability from one technique to another and help smooth the transition to normal speech.

CHORAL RESPONSE

From the very first day of class when the teacher is literally forced to put unfamiliar words into the children's mouths and gradually, in the weeks that follow, elicit them back as familiar responses, choral work is all-important. It is a simple method, benefiting especially the pupils who may hesitate at first to try their pronunciation without the cover afforded by group recitation. In addition to

building confidence, it reinforces the desired sound pattern by permitting the teacher to hear fuzzy or inexact group sound and later, deviations from a good group norm. He may then correct or reteach without isolating any individual child.

Choral response consists quite simply at first in choral repetition by the entire group of children of a sentence or word group pronounced by the teacher acting as linguistic model. The next step may be a stimulus (either a question or a dialogue sentence) that elicits an automatic linguistic reaction from the entire group. Later as the linguistic experience has increased, the class may be divided and the halves act as choral groups for reinforcement practice. Normally the teacher will proceed from total class to smaller group to individual response. In leading the choral response the teacher has certain definite obligations toward the learners. He should pronounce every syllable clearly with good intonation. The teacher must at the same time maintain the right speed while modeling the sentence and must repeat it often enough for the pupils to be able to imitate the sounds. The right speed does not mean a uniform speed without considering the different abilities of the pupils. During the initial stages of teaching new material, parts of sentences, even parts of words must sometimes be isolated to enable pupils to hear correctly. The rest of the sentence will assume the speed of normal conversation.

PATTERN PRACTICE

To the language teacher pattern practice means a drill on some structural patterns basic to the language, for example, a negative form in French. Theoretically a structure drill need not be communication. "It is to communication what playing scales and arpeggios is to music: exercise in structural dexterity undertaken solely for the sake of practice, in order that performance may become habitual and automatic. . . ." [2] However, it is our contention that all pattern practice conducted in the elementary school should be part of a dialogue or be concretely based on some tangible reality, either a group of objects or large reproductions such as classroom language charts, or outsized pictures. For elementary school children, the pattern drill must at least seem to have a definite meaning.

---

[2] Nelson Brooks, *Language and Language Learning* (New York: Harcourt, race & World, Inc., 1960), p. 142.

It must be a form of communication for them to learn the pattern. Very little guesswork should enter into this learning situation. The nature of the construction will determine whether the pupil will understand individual words and phrases or whether he will know just the general meaning of a sentence. The aim of the teacher must always be to encourage repetition on the part of the learner who puts forth a conscious effort to remember rather than to comply with a parrot-like repetition. When the child understands and can attach a new sentence to known material or to a strong visual aid, he will remember longer and more easily. As much time as possible should be spent in learning patterns which differ from those in English since a completely new linguistic habit is being formed.

Simplicity is the keynote in pattern drill. Sentences should be short and the pattern being drilled should be rigid; variety should be provided only by change in vocabulary, for: ". . . *l'apprentissage d'une langue ne consiste pas uniquement dans l'acquisition d'un vocabulaire, mais encore et surtout dans la pratique aisée et courante des formes et des constructions grammaticales usuelles.*" [3] Verbs constitute a major problem in learning a foreign language since their use with the freedom of automaticity involves such a variety of forms; hence, many key sentences expressing action should be taught with pattern practice on change of person and, in the upper elementary grades, on change in time. Since these verbs are always in a sentence or dialogue pattern, the pupil is never conscious of any "camouflaged grammar." He is simply expressing an action in a specific situation. A good course of study will automatically include many verbs rather than a large number of nouns. Attention may be focussed upon the verb by means of a picture, a stick figure, or pupil action. As the teacher moves about the room, he may perform or pantomine actions asking the class to repeat the appropriate expression after him, thus: *Je vais à la fenêtre; je ferme la fenêtre; je vais au bureau; j'ouvre le bureau; je prends un livre;* etc. After the chorus work individual pupils will supply the sentences, each one in turn, as the teacher pantomimes the action. Now the imperative form is introduced and commands may be given to volunteer pupils who perform the action and *accompany their action with the*

---

[3] R. Frété and R. Magne, *Nouvelles Leçons de language*, Premier Livre: C préparatoire des écoles musulmanes (Rabat, Morocco: Direction de l'Instr· Publique, 1954), p. v.

verbal expression of it. The third step is to allow a pupil to take the teacher's place, pantomime the action and say, *Qu'est-ce que je fais?* The response *Tu vas à la fenêtre* is first given by the teacher, then by the class and later by individual pupils. This technique for pattern drill should be used intermittently throughout the elementary grades and continued in junior high school. Pupils who have experienced this type of exercise respond easily to pattern practice as provided by the tape recorder in junior and senior high school laboratories.

Informal pattern practice proves to be very effective and can be included in any day's lesson with little planning by the teacher who can improvise from circumstances or surroundings. A good example might be pattern practice on negatives. Beginning pupils enjoy describing the weather. Immediately after the preliminary class greetings the teacher may turn the "conversation" to the weather. Occasionally he may take advantage of this opportunity to incorporate questions requiring negative answers:

TEACHER: Est-ce qu'il fait mauvais?
CLASS: Non, il ne fait pas mauvais.
TEACHER: Est-ce qu'il pleut?
CLASS: Non, il ne pleut pas.

The teacher may continue thus and at any time move into the day's review and drill by using first the "negative approach" as a means of transition and of linking the drill on negatives to the day's material.

QUESTION AND ANSWERS

One of the most direct and universally used techniques in foreign-language teaching is that of "question-answer." Speciously simple, it may cause even an experienced teacher to frustrate his class when the simple question asked by the teacher either does not supply the vocabulary required in the answer or does not clearly designate the structural pattern. *The child cannot say what he has not been taught to say.* Question-answer technique is useful and valid only with known material, that is, material already drilled chorally or in pattern drill. Its greatest value is as an aid to developing simple easy conversation on topical subjects. It should also give the pupil the ability to formulate the correct question to a given answer as well as the answer to that question. Personal expression through substitution in patterns should be encouraged. This technique may well be used in the following situations:

1. Review questions are appropriate during the "warm-up time" in the beginning of the period. (A discussion of health, the weather, the date, and the day falls into this category.)
2. Familiar material that is designed to lead into a new unit deserves careful review.
3. Review of known material is wise before the teacher introduces a dialogue or scene based on it.

The "question-answer" technique is not limited to the teacher-to-class procedure, but may be used in a number of ways, progressively: teacher to class; teacher to individual pupils; group of pupils to group of pupils; individual to group; and finally individual to individual. Here again, strong visual aids in the form either of a collection of objects (for instance, a furnished doll's house), large pictures or an attractively decorated classroom will provide the external stimulus as well as the extra-linguistic cues needed for an active, meaningful exchange. Well directed question-answer periods may eventually lead to individual "original talks" by pupils on a given topic.

DIALOGUES AND SCENES

Simple conversations, dialogues, and short scenes, or even parts of longer plays provide the teacher with a good medium for teaching language, since it is more meaningful in such contexts than in isolated questions and answers. These scenes take the pupils out of the classroom into an imagined but, nevertheless, realistic situation. The participation in a foreign culture afforded by these scenes helps the children to absorb cultural implications with very little or no explanation in English. Pupils learn to associate a chain of sentences with a definite activity. Thus a sentence has a certain meaning in an imagined situation such as buying a toy in a French store or dramatizing a story.

Some experienced FLES theorists consider the situational dialogue the best means of presentation for new material. According to their theory, the dialogue is memorized to automaticity by the children with little or no consideration for the component parts either from the point of view of meaning or structure. This procedure has proved successful in many programs, but it is our considered judgment that the same dialogue is even more successful where the teacher builds toward it more gradually, drilling the new structural pattern with a variety of drills which will tend to develop a mature understanding of how to handle the structures and a more complete understanding of the meaning without translation. Furthermore, the final result is automaticity on not only the text of the dialogue itself, but on many parallel expressions of thought using the same structures. The child is more at ease because he has *experienced* a wider variety of contexts for a single pattern.

DRAMATIZATIONS

In addition to the pattern drills, dialogues, and short conversations used to present and drill new language material, a further enrichment can be accrued by introducing the dramatization of scenes and stories. This activity evolves quite naturally as the culminating point of and conclusion to a unit or even a series of units. Such a procedure further emphasizes the real-life communication quality of language by means of a simple activity dear to most children: "let's pretend. . . ." These scenes, furthermore, develop leaders in every class, provide the extroverts an opportunity for self-expression and help all those who participate to become more fluent. It has been proved over and over again that a simple dramatization by children in a foreign language will impress a parental or lay audience far beyond its intrinsic value. In the early years of FLES, when such audiences needed convincing to institute or continue a regular FLES program, such "public exhibitions" were occasionally overdone. A judicious use of dramatization for an audience does, however, have educational value and positive personal rewards for the children that should not be neglected nor denigrated.

Such dramatizations may be divided for the convenience of our discussion into two types, known and unknown. The categories are by no means absolute and simplicity remains the keynote to both.

Known Dramatizations. A simple dramatization, which may be used toward the end of each unit, is created by giving various children the opportunity to act out for the class the unit they have been studying. All the accepted FLES manuals are constructed in situational units providing linguistic communication centered upon some topic. Whatever the subject, the children will enjoy performing for their classmates. In such situations the audience should be urged to be constructively critical, aiding in case of memory lapse on the part of the actor, criticizing pronunciation, intonation, and diction after the performance.

As the year progresses both the teacher and the children will want to "strike out" beyond the rigid text. This must be done with care of course, but new situations may be created by recombining known material. For example, after the children have learned the patterns for illnesses, *J'ai mal à la tête.* . . etc., the daily greeting sequence may be varied from *Très bien merci, et toi?* to a realistic discussion of health—or hunger or whatever the child may be inspired to substitute from his other patterns. Such substitution is both creative and spontaneous use of language in a real life situation.

The third level in this dramatization of known material may be effected when the teacher and the class build together a short narrative story situation. Volunteer actors may then, in the best *commedia dell'arte* tradition, supply their own dialogue from their known patterns. The inevitable digressions which intrude themselves either from the child's spontaneity or his sincere misunderstanding of contextual meaning will serve as signals to the teacher of the progress of the class or the need to review. This particular kind of dramatization has a gamelike quality which children enjoy at the same time that it challenges them to use their French spontaneously.

Unknown Dramatizations. Dramatization of material not already familiar to the children must be undertaken with great care and, in general, consumes precious time far out of proportion to its inherent value. Even public performances should grow out of the classroom linguistic patterns. The educational value to the child must always take precedence over the teacher's pride in the rote-memory ability of the child. By the same token, costumes and "props" should be kept to a minimum: what is required to give the dialogue realism (for example, a gift, if a child is handing un *cadeau* to another child) or a single piece of costuming that identifies a character and symbolizes the total costume (for example, a hat = le *père*; an apron = la *mère*, etc.).

Upon occasion, nevertheless, there is real educational value and challenge in choosing to dramatize a story that is apparently quite outside the children's daily classroom activity. This difference needs to be more apparent than real, however, for the story content should still be familiar to the children like "The Three Bears" for young children or "Sleeping Beauty" for older children.[4] Both of these stories and many others have, in addition to the advantage of a known story line, much dialogue which is not different from the language patterns the children have been learning in class (for instance, *Cette chaise est grande; cette chaise est petite;* etc.). Every effort should be made to incorporate the pattern into the story so that in the end the new linguistic material is reduced to a minimum. In the case of "The Three Bears," the children will need to learn the noun *l'ours* and the adjective *moyen* as key words; perhaps ten other incidental, nonobligatory phrases will also be necessary. It is obvious that the story can best be taught after the units on the family, the house, and food.

Such dramatization functions best as a "camouflaged review" offering the challenge of a new context for known responses. It has further value and stimulation when the children can exhibit their attainments to an appreciative audience in a school assembly or to a parent group. The audience's possible lack of linguistic comprehension is compensated for by the familiar story line. It must be repeated, however, that *simplicity*, together with a high percentage of dialogue that can be transferred from previous activities into a new context, is the keynote to success in such a production. The new material should, furthermore, be introduced to the class by choral response, pattern drill, etc., just as if this were merely a new unit of teaching.

A very good game for teaching a long and troublesome sentence is "Locomotive." The sentence is repeated in chorus very slowly, gradually increasing the tempo to very rapid, then decreasing again. By the time the children have said it that many times, they have learned it.

In upper elementary grades, a dramatization may be used for what we call "concentric planning." Concentric planning is simply a means of reviewing a unit taught in the first or second year but now also adding to it new patterns and more vocabulary than was first taught. A Christmas scene, for example, may be essentially the

---

[4] The teacher is referred to *Mon Livre* by E. F. Gessler (1956) for short scenes which may be used in elementary and junior high programs. The book may be obtained from Gessler Publishing Company, 110 East 23d Street, New York 10, New York.

same for three years, but evolving linguistically each year as the children are able to handle easily more dialogue about the Christmas story. Thus what the sixth grader might say will be, in part, comprehensible to a fourth grader and even more, but not totally, comprehensible to a fifth grader.

The teaching of all material should be channeled as much as possible into conversations and dialogues or dramatized scenes, but since these activities hold varying degrees of interest for classes, they should never be forced on a particular class that resists them strongly. It seems quite reasonable to expect every class to learn thoroughly a certain number of conversations or dramatized scenes a year. Since each class possesses a personality with likes and dislikes, however, their preference has to be taken into consideration. One class may be weak in conversation but strong in aural comprehension, use of numbers, solving of problems, or answering questions. Such a class can be encouraged to talk more. As the self-confidence of the individual pupils increases, they will participate to a greater extent in conversational activities.

Variations in procedures will prevent boredom and fatigue, for children enjoy these different activities. "Variety fosters interest. This does not mean variety for the sake of variety, but variety for the sake of mental and physical stimulation." [5] We are stimulating the children to use a reasonable amount of language creatively. They are working with basic patterns, which are all too often used by rote; but in dramatized scenes the child will learn to form new combinations and substitutions which open up a new horizon to his use of the language.

---

[5] Frank A. Butler, *Improvement of Teaching in Secondary Schools* (Chicago: University of Chicago Press, 1954), p 161.

Chapter IV

Planning the Lesson

In Chapter III, we considered the techniques to be used in the presentation and drill of new material. We have also seen that language learning is, in large measure, habit formation and cumulative. What is learned on the first day must be systematically reviewed and used to remain vital at the active level of the child's linguistic consciousness. Planning the individual lesson therefore takes on a very special importance so that within the twenty-minute or half-hour period allotted to language instruction, some constant, equitable balance is kept for review, drill, and the presentation of new material. These pressures should not, however, result in a completely ossified pattern of monotonous routine. The teacher is encouraged to use his originality in adjusting the material to the interests and capacities of the individual class, to secure the appropriate audio-visual teaching aids, and by creative planning to make each separate class a challenging, satisfying, and thoroughly enjoyable experience for the pupils.

Obviously motivation is of supreme importance. Interest may be stimulated by clever presentation of new material, by enthusiasm demonstrated for the pupil's achievement, by a wise use of conversations and scenes, by choice of attractive visual displays and interesting audial aids for use at the most propitious time, by integrating cultural units with language teaching, and by a convincing correlation with other subjects in the curriculum. And yet with all this, the balance of the linguistic elements must have a commanding priority in the planning.

The importance of pace, moreover, cannot be overemphasized. After taking into consideration the capabilities of a particular group the teacher must set the appropriate pace and maintain it insofar as possible. Thus a fast, stimulating pace may be excellent for some classes, but a slower, steadier tempo might be preferable for others. If the forward movement of the class is either too fast or too slow the teacher risks the possibility of losing part of the group. Pupils become discouraged and lose interest if they cannot keep up with the pace. They become bored if things move too slowly. A simple Comprenez-vous? from the teacher, after which a pupil may be called upon to give an example which is rewarded by an encouraging word or two, may be sufficient for the slower student, bright students will require extra challenge. A skillful teacher will change pace easily with various activities; his aims in doing so are to keep the children alert, maintain interest, and use the time as efficiently as possible. Flexibility of technique is essential to good teacher planning; variety of procedure and change of pace are merely two phases of flexibility.

Good planning involves the overall consideration of a unit containing individual lesson plans in continuous succession. One lesson is not an entity in itself. In planning a week's work the teacher must decide which methods are best suited to achieve the objectives of the unit or series of lessons and which props or audio-visual aids will be needed. Whatever his procedures, the teacher will want to be sure that one activity follows another in logical sequence. The cumulative aspect of language learning should be ever present in the teacher's planning.

The following work is an example of unit planning and also of the cumulative or inter-locking quality of two units. These units follow each other, and a plan in which unit A is reviewed and enlarged is presented for the next year. The main objective of these units is to teach the agreement and placement of adjectives through their use in a classroom situation and to drill the singular forms of *montrer*. At the same time the pattern is constantly being manipulated.

In the first year an entire unit is devoted to the teaching of colors and their use in familar and new structural patterns.

UNIT A: LES COULEURS

Step 1. Presentation of three basic colors:

Voilà le *drapeau américain*.
Le drapeau américain est *rouge*, *blanc*, et *bleu*.
(The teacher points to each color as he says it.)
De quelle couleur est le drapeau américain?
(The answer is given first, the question is asked, then the answer is taught.)
Voilà le drapeau *français*.
Le drapeau français est bleu, blanc, et rouge.
De quelle couleur est le drapeau français?

Step 2. Review and presentation of additional colors:

Le papier est *vert*.
Le papier est *jaune*.
Le papier est *marron*.
Le papier est *noir*.

(Each time, the teacher points to a piece of paper of the color he is naming. He may continue with any number of colors on subsequent days, but two or three new ones will suffice at a time.)

Step 3. Drill:

Touche le papier noir.
Montre le papier jaune.
Où est le papier vert?
Est-ce bleu? Oui, c'est bleu.
Non, ce n'est pas bleu. C'est rouge.

Step 4. Game activity:

Jeu de devinette, oui et non. A pupil leaves the room, the class chooses an object and the pupil must guess what has been chosen. Example:
Pupil: Est-ce le papier noir?
Class: Non, ce n'est pas le papier noir.
Pupil: Est-ce le crayon vert?
Class: Oui, c'est le crayon vert.

Subsequent class periods will be spent reviewing and drilling the colors. The feminine forms of the adjectives will be introduced contrastively with the masculine forms and by using visible objects.

Step 2a. Identification of colors:

> Qu'est-ce qui est rouge dans la classe? bleu? blanc?
> Le corsage est blanc.
> La chemise est *blanche.*
> Le papier est vert.
> La robe est *verte.*

Step 3a. Drill: Using a sheet upon which have been pasted pictures of different colored dresses, the teacher provides plenty of drill on the feminine forms *verte, blanche, grise,* and *violette.*

> La robe est blanche.
> La chemise aussi est blanche.
> La table est verte.
> La gomme aussi est verte.
> La *plante* est verte.
>
> Combien de couleurs est-ce que tu connais?
>
> One pupil names the colors in French and says:
>
> Je connais onze couleurs.
> Combien de crayons rouges? Cinq crayons rouges.
> Combien de papiers blancs? Trois papiers blancs.
> Mets le papier rouge sur la table; sur le papier blanc.
> Je mets le papier rouge sur la table.

Step 4a. Game activity:

> Je vois quelque chose de marron dans la classe. Qu'est-ce que c'est?
> Est-ce le pantalon?
> Oui, c'est le pantalon marron.

The next unit deals with two new adjectives, the verb *montrer,* and a few new nouns. The adjectives *gros* and *petit* which modify nouns in both masculine and feminine forms are introduced. The children have already encountered the idea of inflection in the unit on colors. Structural patterns using all the singular forms of *montrer* and one imperative form of *donner,* both new and very useful verbs, are used. The imperative and first singular have been learned for *toucher, écrire, compter,* and *mettre* in previous units. In this presentation, the second and third persons singular are also taught as new material.

UNIT B: NEW ADJECTIVES AND VERBS

Step 1. Presentation:

Montre le *gros* chien.
Je montre le gros chien.
Oui, tu montres le gros chien.
TOUT LE MONDE: *Il* montre le gros chien.
Donne-moi le gros chien s'il te plaît.
Voici le gros chien.
Montre le *petit* chien.
Je montre le petit chien.
Oui, tu montres le petit chien.
TOUT LE MONDE: *Elle* montre le petit chien.
Mets le petit chien sur la table.
Je mets le petit chien sur la table.

Step 2. Drill:

De quelle couleur est la petite balle?
La petite balle est blanche.
Mets la *petite balle blanche* sur la chaise.
Je mets la petite balle blanche sur la chaise.
Donne-moi la petite gomme verte.
Voici la petite gomme verte.

Step 3. Game activity:

Using white construction paper, cut out outlines of various
animals which the children know such as: *le chat, le chien,
l'éléphant, le lapin, le poisson.* Place the pattern against colored paper to produce various colored animals and say:
Je montre un éléphant orange, etc. (Then give the command
to a pupil:)
Montre un chien rouge.
Mets le chien rouge sur la table.
Donne le chien rouge à Marie.

The teacher will need to adapt this type of unit to the needs of
his individual classes and to prepare the necessary visual materials.
As the pupils learn the new vocabulary and structural patterns
adequate drill must be provided. The game described holds the
children's interest because it encourages active participation and
provides opportunities to use the new structural patterns.

A general review should be conducted in the beginning of the
second year. Such a review unit might look something like the

following. The unit begins with a game that provides strong incentive to recall. It continues with various patterns and sentences of increasing complication from a structural point of view.

REVIEW UNIT: SECOND YEAR

Step 1. Game:

J'ai cinq couleurs derrière le dos.
Dis une couleur.
After an individual pupil has guessed a color, the teacher shows one of the five colors. If the pupil has not guessed correctly, the teacher says, *Non, ce n'est pas le rouge. C'est le vert.* Later a pupil takes the teacher's place in leading this game.

Step 2. Colors are used in these structural patterns:

Montre le gros chat noir.
Montre un petit chat gris.
Montre une grosse boîte blanche.
Montre le petit poisson rouge.

Step 3. Drill on the plural:

Montre les boîtes, les pastels.
Donne-moi les boîtes, les pastels bleus.
Où sont les boîtes jaunes?
Touche, prends les papiers blancs, les boîtes blanches.

Step 4. Choosing animals:

Quel animal aimes-tu?
J'aime l'éléphant violet.
Donne l'éléphant violet à Marie.

Step 5. Identification of colors: Eleven pupils are in front of the class holding colored objects. Another pupil says, *Montre-moi le papier vert.*

Step 6. Finding colors:

Qu'est-ce qui est blanc dans la classe?
Quelle chose est blanche dans la classe?
These questions will refer to any object, picture, or article of clothing that has been learned.

Step 7. Voluntary descriptions: Some pupils choose animal cutouts and place them on colored sheets. They show them to the class and describe their animals.

Step 8. Pupils form sentences in response to questions:

Est-ce que le chat est gros?

De quelle couleur est le gros chat?
Le gros chat est gris.
Le petit lapin est brun.
La grosse boîte est verte.
La petite balle est rouge, blanche, et bleue.
Où est la gomme verte?
Voici la gomme verte.

The daily lessons of each unit should be planned with care. One item essential to good planning is the systematic re-introduction of review material. The most efficient method of finding enough time to review old conversations and to teach new units at the same time can become a real problem to the beginning teacher as the children progress through their second, third, and fourth years of FLES—a problem which is solved, however, in a well-written elementary course. "This integration of new and review may be compared to moving in an upward spiral in which each turn around the circle pulls in and combines new material with review. Going round and round in the same circle is as much to be avoided as going forward in a straight line and forgetting everything but the current vocabulary areas." [1] The work taught in the first year is picked up again during the second year; it is further developed and later reappears in a dialogue or in the form of a story and is finally read.

Language learning requires concentrated effort which is best relieved by occasional humor. Laughter reduces tension and the strain of prolonged, attentive listening. The more they laugh, the more they learn. It renders this arduous mental work more enjoyable. The foreign-language teacher must not fail to remember this. Here are two suggestions which may be used as skeletal outlines in planning any lesson. They can be adapted to the unit material in order to maintain continuity. Most lessons which do not involve dialogues and which are taught during the first year may be planned according to one of these outlines. Of course, modifications should be made to suit the occasion.

SKELETAL PLAN I

I. Motivation: The direct attack. Present new material with good "props" or visual aids. The pupils repeat new vocabulary as a group and individually. In the second year the day's lesson may be intro-

---

[1] Margit MacRae, *Teaching Spanish in the Grades* (Boston: Houghton Mifflin Company, 1957), pp. 21–22.

duced with *Aujourd'hui nous allons parler de* . . . followed by an introduction of the new subject. This statement is within their understanding because it uses vocabulary which has been taught at a previous date. No further preparation is necessary in most instances.

II. Development:

    A. Simple identification of new nouns (indefinite article is used), usually concrete objects or people.

    B. Use of new vocabulary in several other familiar speech patterns.

III. Review of familiar material to increase confidence and encourage a feeling of achievement. A song or a game might be used here as an alternate activity.

IV. Review of the new vocabulary and speech patterns with the class. The teacher may say, *Et maintenant, une petite révision.* . . . He then proceeds to review the new vocabulary and sentence patterns. He may allow the class to say them with him or he may encourage individual pupils to show that they have already mastered the new material. This affords them an opportunity for self-expression and gives them a feeling of accomplishment. It also helps the whole class to retain the new material.

V. Question time: The teacher asks, *Y a-t-il des questions?* and the pupils are allowed to ask questions. Thus the teacher may clear up any possible misunderstanding. The child's question may be asked and answered in English, but if the question falls under the category of an expression or pattern that has been taught, he is asked to repeat it in French. This may be done with the aid of the teacher and class. The class will normally come quite naturally to ask these questions in French. For the purpose of avoiding monotony it is advisable to allow question time only once a week.

VI. Note: The next day it is best to review all the new material first.

LESSON PREPARED ACCORDING TO SKELETAL PLAN I

I. The teacher presents the exterior of the house using a cardboard model of a French house (*maison préfabriquée avec ses meubles*), or a large picture with the following introduction: Voici une *maison* française. Il y a deux arbres devant la maison. Voilà le *toit*. Le toit est rouge. Il y a deux cheminées. Les cheminées sont rouges. Voilà le *mur*, les murs. Je montre les *volets*. Le *jardin* est ici.

II. A. Est-ce une maison? Oui, c'est une maison.

    Montre-moi la porte de la maison.

    Où est le toit de la maison?

    Montre le mur, quatre murs.

    Touche un arbre, deux arbres.

Combien y a-t-il de cheminées?
De quelle couleur est le toit?
Où est le toit? Le toit est sur la maison.
Y a-t-il des volets? Oui, il y a des volets.
Où sont les volets? Voici les volets.
Touche une fenêtre de la maison. Je. . . .
Où est une fenêtre de la salle de classe? Voilà. . . .
Montre le jardin. Je montre le jardin.

B. As-tu une maison?
De quelle couleur est ta maison? Ma. . . .
As-tu un jardin, un arbre, des arbres, des volets, une porte?
De quelle couleur est la porte de ta maison?

III. Qui veut compter par dix?
Écris le numéro soixante sur le tableau, soixante-cinq, soixante-neuf, soixante-six, soixante-quatre, soixante-dix, soixante-et-un.
Marie, vas au tableau. Montre soixante-cinq. Efface soixante-dix.
Ecris soixante-quatorze. Où est soixante-six? Touche soixante-et-un.
This game may be played at this point: Soixante, soixante-et-un, soixante-trois. Qu'est-ce qui manque? Il manque soixante-deux.

IV. Et maintenant, une petite révision. (Pointing to the house) C'est une (maison). (The class supplies the word *maison*.) Je touche le (mur de la maison), etc. Demain nous allons parler d'une maison américaine.

SKELETAL PLAN II

I. Preparing pupils for new material.
A. Greeting and weather.
B. A few stock expressions which are easily forgotten or confused if they are not used constantly. One dialogue may be reviewed for a few weeks or until it has been well learned.

II. Review of old material which leads directly into the presentation of the new.

III. Presentation of new subject matter.

IV. A challenging activity to stimulate the use of the new material. This activity may consist of humorous contradictory questions which are very effective. There may be a contest between two teams which provides repetitive drill. Familiar vocabulary may be interspersed with the new. This will prompt the entire class to think in the language.

V. The relaxing part of the lesson could consist of a song, a game, or some number work. The song or game should be related to the material taught whenever possible

LESSON PREPARED ACCORDING TO
SKELETAL PLAN II

Since new material has been introduced which should be reviewed as soon as possible, it is to be expected that the second lesson on the house might be planned according to Skeletal Plan II. Two class periods may even be necessary for the children to learn the new vocabulary thoroughly, as just naming the parts will not suffice. They must use the various constructions as indicated.

HOUSE AND FAMILY: FIRST YEAR

I. A. Bonjour, tous. Comment allez-vous?
        Comment vas-tu, Jean?
        Quel temps fait-il aujourd'hui?
  B. Quel jour est-ce aujourd'hui?
        Comment t'appelles-tu? Comment s'appelle-t-il?
        Compte de douze à vingt-cinq.
        Ouvre un livre. Ferme le livre. Donne-moi le livre, s'il te plaît.

II. A. Ouvre la porte, la fenêtre.
        Review of parts of the house. Then:
        Touche le mur dans la salle de classe.
        Combien y a-t-il demurs?
        Où est le plancher?
        Combien y a-t-il de portes, de fenêtres dans la classe?
  B. Teacher shows a picture of an American house and calls for a quick identification of the new vocabulary.

III.   Quelle est la différence entre la maison américaine et la maison française? La maison française a un toit rouge et deux cheminées. La maison américaine a une cheminée. Le toit n'est pas rouge. Il est gris. (A picture of a typical French house is shown in contrast to the American house.)

IV.   Voulez-vous jouer? Nous allons avoir un "match" entre les deux équipes.
The classes can be divided into two teams and the cumulative score is kept. Sometimes individual names or initials are written for each point scored. In questions of identity three objects must be named correctly in order to gain a point. All questions from both lessons may be included here and the following humorous, contradictory questions may be added:
As-tu un arbre dans le salon, un piano dans le jardin, deux cheminées sur le toit, un toit rouge?

Plan II is more widely used than Plan I because it is more practical and logical. It takes some pupils a little more time to readjust their thinking to French. They listen attentively for old familiar questions and recognize familiar procedures which help to give them some feeling of security. They haven't thought about or spoken one French word since the last time the FLES teacher visited their room. The change from one subject to another is necessarily abrupt because of the pressure of finding time in which to teach all the subjects in the elementary curriculum. The medium used in teaching all other subjects is, of course, English, but the medium of the foreign-language class is essentially the foreign language. Therefore, it seems more practical to conduct a partial review and to construct a foundation upon which the new lesson will securely rest. The known material should be established first, after which the teacher can proceed to the unknown.

Succeeding lessons on the house will be limited in the first year to learning the rooms of the house, one or two articles of furniture in each room and several statements about playing in the garden. A French family will live in the French house and an American family in the American home. Plans for teaching this material might include such items as follows:

I.   A house may be constructed by placing cutouts of the various parts of a house against a piece of galvanized sheet iron with the help of magnets. The teacher will demonstrate the use of this teaching aid before calling upon individual pupils: Voici les *parties* de la maison. Je mets le mur. Je mets le toit. *J'enlève* le toit. Voulez-vous répéter les parties de la maison? . . . Jean, mets la porte. Mireille, mets deux fenêtres, etc.

II. The parts of the house may also be reviewed by directing pupils to draw and erase them at the board.

III. Il y a cinq *pièces* dans la maison: *le salon, la salle à manger, la cuisine, une chambre à coucher, et la salle de bain.* (Pictures may be used to show the various rooms.)

IV. One or two pieces of furniture can be identified with each room.
   A. Le *canapé* est dans le salon. La cheminée aussi est dans le salon.
   B. Il y a une table et des chaises dans la salle à manger.
   C. La *cuisinière* est dans la cuisine.
   D. Voici le *lit* dans la chambre à coucher.
   E. Le *lavabo* est dans la salle de bain.

V.   Que *fais-tu* dans le jardin?
       Je joue dans le jardin.
       Je *saute* à la corde.
       Je joue à la balle, au ballon.
       Je joue aux *billes*.

VI.   This cumulative story, which begins with a house, may be presented by a series of nine pictures: *L'histoire suivie "du lapin à la maison."*[2]

    A. Voilà la maison.
    B. Voilà la porte de la maison.
    C. Voilà la *clef* qui ouvre la porte de la maison.
    D. Voilà la *dame* qui tourne . . .
    E. Voilà le chapeau de la dame . . .
    F. Voilà la fleur qui est sur . . .
    G. Voilà le jardin où pousse la fleur . . .
    H. Voilà le lapin qui habite le jardin . . .
    I. Voilà le chien qui *chasse* le lapin qui habite le jardin où pousse la fleur qui est sur le chapeau de la dame qui tourne la clef qui ouvre la porte de la maison.

VII.   Qui habite la maison?
       Une *famille* habite la maison.
       Voilà la famille.
       La famille s'appelle *Gilles*.
       Voilà le père. Il s'appelle Monsieur Gilles.
       Voilà la mère. Elle s'appelle Madame Gilles.
       Le garçon s'appelle Max. C'est le frère.
       Voilà une petite fille qui s'appelle Monique. C'est la *soeur* de Max.
       Il y a quatre personnes dans la famille.
       Qui est Monsieur Gilles? Monsieur Gilles est le père, etc.
       Qui est-ce? C'est la mère.

The study of the house is an inexhaustible subject. Care should be exercised lest too much time be spent on one unit, thereby losing the interest of the pupils. The objective of the entire series of lessons on the house is to talk about daily living in the house and not to learn a large number of nouns. Additional material will be presented in this interesting area in the future. Thus we are not moving forward in a straight line, forgetting each unit a short time after it has been learned. Because of our concentric planning we will

---

[2] Permission granted by the Gessler Publishing Co. for use of this story.

return to the study of the house during the second year with its built-in necessity for review. The elementary pupil readily understands the need for reviewing the subject matter of the preceding year.

LA CHAMBRE A COUCHER ET LA SALLE DE BAIN

The bedroom and the bathroom are presented at the same time on a chart or a large picture which has been made to order. Cutouts of people and objects should stand out boldly against the background.

    I. The words *le pyjama, un lit,* and *le lavabo* are reviewed. The expressions *montre, touche, où est* . . . are used with these nouns and old vocabulary suggested by the chart.

    II. Y a-t-il un lit, un plancher, une table, un avion dans ta chambre?
Il y a . . .
Il n'y a pas de . . .

    III. These actions are taught by dramatization:
Qu'est-ce que tu fais dans la chambre?
Je mets mon pyjama.
Je me couche (dans mon lit).
Je dors.
Je me lève.

    IV. A quelle heure est-ce que to mets ton pyjama? . . . tu te couches?
. . . tu dors? . . . tu te lèves?

    V. One day the teacher brings into class these props: a small mirror, a comb, a towel, soap, a toothbrush and French toothpaste. These nouns are taught: *une glace, un peigne, une serviette, le savon, une brosse à dents, et le dentifrice.*

    VI. These actions are taught by dramatization:
Je me lave les mains avec du savon et de l'eau.
Je me rince les mains avec de l'eau.
Je m'essuie les mains avec la serviette.
Je me brosse les dents avec la brosse et le dentifrice.

    VII. The teacher pantomimes the action and asks:
Quelle est la phrase pour cette action? Deux points pour les phrases difficiles dans le concours.

    VIII. Questions of place:
Où est-ce que tu te laves les mains?
Je me lave les mains dans le lavabo dans la salle de bain.
Où est-ce que tu mets ton pyjama?
. . . tu regardes la télévision?

Note: As mentioned before, a contest is held. Three identification questions must be answered to gain one point. For every other sentence spoken correctly one point is given. A cumulative record is kept until the study of the house has been finished. Pupils may ask each other questions in the contest. These lessons on the various rooms of the house illustrate a method by which the teacher can aim the discussion at three different levels of learning, namely, disguised repetition, identification of objects, and the composition of sentences.

In this way total participation can be effected by using questions to be aimed at different levels of achievement. It is important to know to which group in the class the question is being directed.

I. Disguised repetition. Choral work may be used here by having the entire class ask a question for individual response or by having one pupil ask a question of the class. *Est-ce un lavabo?* is an example of this type of question. The telling of time, which may be studied in connection with the house unit, lends itself easily to this technique. These questions are prompted by the teacher.

II. Identification of objects which is self-explanatory. Here a certain pattern of speech is used by the teacher who then says, *Qui veut prendre ma place?* The extrovert who loves to perform can easily take his place and ask similar questions of his classmates. When a pupil asks the question, *Est-ce un lit?* requiring a negative answer, he is clearly demonstrating his ability to manipulate the language.

III. Practical application of vocabulary and speech patterns. These responses involve the actual construction of sentences. The pupil is applying what he has learned in a concrete situation. He is responding to verbal stimuli and is able to substitute one word for another within a certain pattern, remembering the form which his answer should take. When he is asked, *Qu'est-ce que c'est?* he will not answer, *Voilà la porte* but *C'est une porte.* When asked how many windows there are in the room, he will not say, *trois fenêtres* but *Il y a trois fenêtres dans la classe.* When asked, *De quelle couleur est . . .?* he will not repeat part of the question. Instead he will put the sentence together.

"No learning of importance ever comes without important activity on the party of the learner. Every important ability demands its proportionate amount of self-activity. Without the price in terms of self-activity, valuable abilities cannot become one's possession."[3]

---

[3] Frank A. Butler, *Improvement of Teaching in Secondary Schools* (Chicago: University of Chicago Press, 1954), p. 57.

The procedures described under planning are only suggestions. In order to teach successful units on the house over a period of several years it is not necessary to do everything suggested. Learning a small amount of material well is better than being vaguely familiar with many things.

Chapter V

Techniques for Teaching
Reading & Writing

Although the primary objective of a foreign-language program in the elementary school is to develop audio-lingual mastery of a minimum vocabulary and some of the basic speech patterns, we believe that sixth grade pupils are ready for a carefully controlled amount of reading and writing. They are usually curious about the written language, and perhaps they need the kind of respect one gets for a language when one learns to write it. If they are not given this further experience while curiosity and interest are high, the normal rate of progress may be delayed.

Sixth grade marks the transition from elementary learning to the kind of study required in the secondary school in all curriculum areas, including foreign languages. However, there is very little agreement among foreign-language teachers upon the best time to begin this transition and the best methods and materials for implementing it. According to one source: "In shifting from audio-lingual work to reading, they have searched, almost in vain, for materials which would effect the transfer with the minimum break in continuity. Another problem has been that of deciding when the transition should be made."[1]

It seems more practical to consider both the sixth and the seventh grades as a period of transition. In fact testing and the use of the printed word in whatever form are very closely related areas at this stage of development. Before the children have reached the age of eleven we make use of their capacity to imitate sounds and reproduce new phrase-rhythms, thus building a sound foundation of audio-lingual achievement. The introduction of reading and writing should be made in the interest of furthering a process already well begun.

Reading should be taught solely to supplement the audio-lingual learning; it is never the medium used in teaching new material. Copying can be used as an aid to memory. Thus the transition to the learning activities of the seventh and eighth grades has begun. The pupil's proficiency in reading and writing is developed increasingly as he moves to the eighth and ninth grades but the development of these skills never replaces oral communication in the foreign language in the classroom. The rest of this discussion will be devoted to the specific use of reading in sixth grade French. The teaching of reading and writing in a foreign language has one very important difference from learning these skills in English. The child has already learned the muscular coordination required; he has "been through all this" once. The only problem involved, therefore, are those inherent in the language itself and in our method of teaching it.

French vies with English or runs a close second as the language with the most inept system of graphics or spelling. There are many silent letters, multiple ways of spelling a sound, and a system of accents which signal the quality of the vowel and not the stress. With the older students such a system leads almost inevitably to what some teachers call the period of "spelling pronunciation." This is a disease which invades classes of maturer students, even when trained audio-lingually, at the first sight of the printed word: they tend to pronounce the letters they see rather than recognize another form of an already familiar word. For this reason, sixth grade children should not be rushed into great quantities of reading, they

---

[1] Frederick B. Agard and Harold B. Dunkel, *An Investigation of Second-Language Learning* (Boston: Ginn & Company, 1948), p 297.

should read only what they already know, and most particularly the teacher should profit from this exercise to review and redrill sound habits of pronunciation.

A second pitfall in teaching reading and writing is a matter of teacher planning. The explanations and drills entailed by reading and writing can very quickly absorb the whole 20 or 30 minute period. Such an imbalance not only stops progress in the audio-lingual skills but favors spelling pronunciation since the child does not hear the familiar sounds during each class period. The easiest and most efficient transition is made when reading and writing are added to hearing and speaking and when every class continues to devote a fair portion of time to these last two skills. "[Reading] is a continuation of the oral expression of the elementary language program."[2] The eye becomes a factor in fixing that which has already been learned making it more tangible and definite. Thus the pupils are reviewing familiar material and recording it for future reference.

Three procedures with many possibilities of variation have become almost standard for this new adjustment to the written word. They are, furthermore, well adapted to the need of the sixth grade child for controlled advance and change in his language learning procedure. The first of these procedures is the introduction of notebooks. Before the class, the teacher has written on the blackboard with special care for clarity not more than five lines of a very simple dialogue learned early in the language study and known to automaticity by the entire class (for example, the daily greetings). After drilling the class again on this material with no reference to the blackboard, the teacher may then bring the written form to the pupils' attention by reading it aloud to and with them—audio-lingual plus visual. The pupils will then copy it carefully into their notebooks and "read" it aloud again in chorus.

Some teachers prefer written legends with pictures which can be discussed without "reading or writing" for as long as the teacher deems necessary to ensure the association of the written form to the oral maintaining the dominance of the latter. In this situation, how-

---

[2] F. C. Peloro, "Report of Working Committee III, Elementary and Junior High School Curricula," *Northeast Conference on the Teaching of Foreign Languages, 1960: Reports of the Working Committees*, Frederick D. Eddy, ed. (Washington, D. C.: Georgetown University, 1959), p. 37.

ever, the copying procedure still requires the same care and drill as in the first instance.

Other pages in the notebook may be devoted to writing numbers, the days of the week, the months of the year, and to telling one's birthday. Questions and answers, also commands and their responses that are basic to the course of study may be included. Pupils are expected to read the material they have written in their notebooks. Class progress may be determined by ability to read what has been written. If drill is needed here, it should be provided. This writing and reading serve the purpose of clinching or clarifying what they have already learned orally and acts as an aid to memory. ". . . reading becomes, as has been stressed repeatedly, the process of recognizing the printed symbol for an already familiar sound." [3] Writing as an aid to study need not necessarily prevent the teacher from introducing new units. A discussion of vacations is conducted in the beginning of the year and constitutes some of the first sentences written. Although some of the vocabulary is familiar, the basic discourse patterns are new. When the new patterns have been thoroughly learned, they are copied into the notebooks.

A second procedure, frequently used in conjunction with notebooks and copying, offers a slightly different approach in that it emphasizes reading without writing. Pupils may be given duplicated copies of dialogues they have learned which they then "read" in unison with the teacher. They thus learn to associate the written forms of the sentences with those they have already learned to automaticity. This process is considered the beginning of reading. The dialogues should be very simple and very short at first. They are usually stapled in the children's notebooks. Some teachers may prefer to have them kept in loose-leaf notebooks. Pupils should not be asked to read too much nor to read silently. The major portion of the classwork should consist of talking and not reading. The French class does not suddenly become a reading class or a class in grammar.

This reading-writing period has been found by experience to be an excellent moment to reteach the sounds of French, the alphabet, and to develop some basic knowledge of the association between

---

[3] Margit MacRae, *Teaching Spanish in the Grades* (Boston: Houghton Mifflin Company, 1957), p. 182.

sounds and their spelling. Such work in phonics is the third procedure usually accompanying the first two. Some experienced FLES
teachers even prefer to begin with this work before using notebooks,
but, in our opinion, care must be exercised not to fragment unduly
the child's sentence pattern into meaningless noises in which he will
quickly lose interest.

In one teacher's manual an entire unit is devoted to teaching of
sounds. Most of the French sounds are presented as a means of
helping the pupils identify certain spelling with familiar sounds and
words. In this way one week's work is devoted to a form of recapitu-
lation. The pupils write twelve of the seventeen vowel sounds
through their spelling equivalents. Individual sounds are isolated in
familiar words and pronounced carefully; attention is given to the
position of the lips and tongue. The words listed as examples of
the various sounds should be discussed as they are written. Some
English may be needed for the purpose of clarity. Children have
an opportunity to detect these sounds in the names of their classmates. The teacher may say *Quel est le nom d'un garçon avec le
son "a"?* and a pupil will suggest *Albert.* Pupils will notice the final
consonants in the words *Roger, Richard, manger, et,* and *vingt* are
not pronounced.

Pupils may volunteer words for the lists. Any incorrect answer
gives the teacher an excellent opportunity to improve faulty pronunciation. Some words and expressions that have been used frequently are now called to the pupils' attention for meaning, for
example, while talking about words containing the sound "*i*," the
teacher will say *Comment dit-on "quickly" en français?* and *vite* is
added to the list. *Marie est une petite fille. Où est le son "i"? . . .
Dites-moi le nom d'un garçon dans la classe avec le son "i" . . . Oui,
Philippe est correct.* Another useful expression is suggested, *Trouvez
un mot avec le son "o."* These lists are copied by the children into
their notebooks and henceforward the teacher will refer the pupils
to them as means of correcting mistakes in reading pronunciation.
Constant reference to these pages of French sounds when words
are mispronounced will help to solidify good habits of pronunciation
and establish an understanding of some spelling forms of the basic
sounds.

The teacher has probably used the French names for a few letters
of the alphabet as he wrote them—just enough to whet the appetite

of the curious. Now the alphabet is taught in its entirety. Drill on separate letters is provided with flash cards but the aim of mastery is actually achieved through use. Familiar words are spelled as the teacher writes words such as *bonjour, au revoir, les jours, zéro, un million* on the board. The expression *Epelez . . . s'il vous plaît* is used. The vowels are introduced with the sentence, *Les voyelles françaises sont* "a," "e," "i," "o," "u," *et* "y". Repetitive drill is provided by *La Chanson des Voyelles. L'homme pendu,* or the hangman's game, helps the pupils become more familiar with the written form of learned vocabulary while providing an excellent and painless way of teaching a limited amount of spelling. As self-confidence grows all pupils should be given an opportunity to lead this game. Interest runs high and experience has proved that "*l'homme pendu*" never wanes in popularity. The game is used intermittently throughout the year but it *must not be overdone.* Words increase to phrases, then to sentences including negatives and interrogatives. The value of this game is three-fold: it serves as a culmination of alphabet study; it introduces and stamps the written word; it is a highly pleasurable activity.

The orthography of French words is gradually presented to the pupils in small amounts. They are beginning to associate certain spelling with certain sounds. By the end of grade six they are able to sound out and spell a reasonable percentage of the material learned. This technique is valuable in French just as it was in teaching spelling in English. The sentences have been chosen for semantic reasons rather than for structural reasons. The pupils are being prepared for a gradually increasing supplement of reading and writing as they continue their study of French, but the emphasis is still placed upon oral work.

The children's notebooks have become a very practical learning tool, as some conscious drill on pronunciation and reading is done when necessary. Individuals or the whole class often refer to this notebook in order to find an answer they have temporarily forgotten. This kind of activity gives pupils a feeling of security in subject matter by providing something tangible as expressed by many pupils when they are asked to write comments on their study of French. One pupil said, "I like to write in the notebooks and then go over what we wrote." The notebook technique provides greater participation by stimulating pupils to use a good reference, thereby adding another approach to language learning; it also provides satisfaction and enjoyment. The use of this invaluable aid to memory is continued in seventh grade where it provides a basis for review.

Through the activity of writing and then reading what has been written the teachers are laying a foundation for developing skill in reading. Through their study of the alphabet the pupils gain an understanding of some of the differences between English and French vowels and consonants as an aid to correct pronunciation of words. This in turn will lead to sight reading of unfamiliar words. This presentation of French sounds has proved to be a good remedial measure for reverting to the spelling pronunciation. "As his readiness becomes greater and his experience with the written symbol of his spoken vocabulary grows, he can be expected to make generalizations from parts of words and letters in known words and apply them in new situations just as he does in English. Thus he will eventually have the key to pronouncing new and unfamiliar words, but at a more mature stage in his foreign language career." [4]

Experience in the techniques just described has shown that on the whole the introduction of a *controlled* amount of reading and writing has provided an important aid to learning in the sixth grade and a whole new field of interest is opening. Although a small percentage of the pupils do not profit to any great extent from the experience, this situation is taken care of by a screening process between sixth and seventh grades. Since fifth and sixth grade children are in a fluid stage of development, it would be a mistake to weed out the less able pupils too quickly. They ought to have this total experience. Writing is a hurdle which helps to divide the group. It is certainly possible to teach academically talented groups by the audio-lingual method exclusively: this fact has been demonstrated often. If, however, all the teaching is done orally in a heterogeneous sixth grade, there is a great risk of losing the interest of many good students who need a new challenge to learning which is still commensurate with the ability of the average pupil. Reading and writing have also proved to be another means of determining the differences between the children who are linguistically gifted and those who are not.

---

[4] *Ibid.*, p. 187.

Chapter VI

Techniques of
Review & Testing

All good teaching needs to be appraised. We must evaluate the results of our work and we must grade the children. It is understood that foreign language is recognized as a serious subject taught during the school day; and as an accepted part of the curriculum, it is included on the pupil's report. Therefore, it is only normal that the teacher should give each child a grade based upon class work and tests. The pupils themselves have more respect for a subject when they realize that certain standards must be met and tangible goals must be achieved.

Following normal teaching procedure the teacher will conduct a review before giving a test. Of course, review of familiar material is a continuous process in any effective program. Dialogues and old vocabulary are constantly reviewed as such or reused in new situations but the pupils are never allowed to forget them. One pupil expressed a very concise opinion of review when asked to write comments on his study of French. He said, "There should be a variety of things learned each day and reviewed a few days later instead of going over it about two or three times in the same day."

Tests make us more conscious of the quality of our teaching. Although the foreign-language teacher is fully aware of class progress, it is easy to assume that the pupils know more than they actually do or to judge the level of the entire class by the achievement of several leaders. An objective evaluation of work will assist the teacher in being realistic about the amount of material that children are able to retain and use in elementary school and reproduce during the crucial period in seventh grade. There is need to distinguish between comprehension ability and speaking ability; to distinguish between language skills and the learning of culture or development of attitudes. In the words of Elizabeth Keesee, "All aspects of the foreign-language-in-elementary-schools program need to be evaluated in terms of the purposes of the program." [1]

We would make an earnest plea for constant review of the basic structural patterns found in the units previously taught, for the omission of any unnecessary material, (that is, the everyday language of living should be given preference over names of many toys and animals), and for a continuous self-evaluation on the part of the teacher for the purpose of strengthening the entire sequence of foreign-language learning within a given school system.

Even on the elementary level test planning should run concurrently with teaching. Methods often fashion themselves to the kind of evaluation to which the pupils will be subject at the end of a period of time, or this evaluation may reclarify the teacher's aim by checking on the accomplishment of a particular part of that aim. Careful planning is necessary in order that a unit or group of units may be followed by a thorough test which reveals to the teacher how much his pupils have actually learned. All tests will be taken directly from the material that has been taught. They are essentially mastery tests. These activities are the natural outcome of regular class work and should be regarded by the children as part of the normal procedure of any French class. Certain games are good informal testing devices. This procedure mitigates any feeling of nervousness which might otherwise invalidate the results of the test. Quite often the word

---

[1] Cited in E. E. Holt, *Modern Foreign Language in Ohio Elementary Schools* (Columbus, Ohio: State Board of Education, 1962), p 19.

"test" or "*examen*" is not mentioned and the children are not conscious of being tested.

A few principles for giving tests have been developed and subjected to experimental trial. Elementary foreign-language tests are most effective when they are brief. They need not consume precious time which is so badly needed for the presentation of new material. Testing must not be overdone. Another essential characteristic of these tests is their simplicity. There is often just one type of question in the quiz and the questions are arranged in order of difficulty. The class is prepared for the test.

The quizzes that will be discussed have been found effective. It may sometimes be necessary to alter the questions to fit the ability of the class. Flexibility seems to be another prerequisite if these exercises are to be reasonably efficient tools of measurement. The teacher will certainly examine the results of a test when administering the same test to other classes or when planning another test for the same group of children. The teacher should know beforehand what mental processes the pupils must use, then note whether they are reacting as anticipated. Each class has its own way of accepting a test. "The center of gravity is the behavior of the pupils rather than subject matter." [2] In summary, tests used in an elementary program should be based upon the following principles: they must be brief, simple, integrated with the course, planned while teaching; and they should be flexible.

The following tests have been used in first-year classes, (third or fourth grade):

TYPE 1: PATTERN TEST

This type of test provides a nonscientific checking of pupil progress. It is not intended to be objective. Theoretically every pupil should answer a question of identity, one negative question, one question about color, and one in which he obeys a command. The teacher may record a mark which according to his judgment represents the pupil's level of achievement. The children may be told in English that this is a review and that they are expected to do their best. The

---

[2] C. C. Ross, *Measurement in Today's Schools* (Englewood Cliffs, N. J.: Prentice-Hall, Inc., 1947), p. 107.

questions and procedure should be varied somewhat as part of three class periods may be needed to test an entire class. This is a simple recall test of material taught. It may also serve as a test of pronunciation.

A. Est-ce une dinde? Oui, c'est une dinde.
   Est-ce le plancher? Non, ce n'est pas le plancher.
   Est-ce une robe verte? Oui, c'est une robe verte.

B. Qu'est-ce qui est bleu dans la classe?
   La chemise de Robert est bleue.
   Qui a un mouchoir blanc?
   Marie a un mouchoir blanc.

C. Est-ce le drapeau américain?
   Non, ce n'est pas le drapeau américain, c'est le drapeau français.
   Est-ce une chaise?
   Non, ce n'est pas une chaise, c'est le bureau.

D. De quelle couleur est la drapeau français?
   Le drapeau français est bleu, blanc, et rouge.
   De quelle couleur est ta robe?
   Ma robe est jaune.

E. Où est le papier noir?
   Où est le crayon rouge?
   Voici le crayon rouge.

F. Montre le tableau noir. Touche le bureau.
   Voilà le tableau noir. Je touche le bureau. Voilà le papier noir.
   (These questions may be used with any nouns that the children know already.)

Within the same framework of the Pattern Test, the teacher may find variety and challenge by indicating two objects about which the child gives an entire sentence. The teacher may also merely point to two objects.

G. Le stylo et la clef
   Le stylo est gris mais la clef est grise.
   Le corsage et la chemise
   Le corsage est blanc mais la chemise est blanche.

TYPE 2: CONVERSATION TEST

The pupil should be able to choose a conversation from those which have been learned during the first half of the year. The aim of this kind of test is to be sure that every child who is capable is given an opportunity to participate in at least one conversation.

It is important that the teacher encourage each child to perfom according to his ability and interest and that he maintain a reasonably good pace at the same time. The teacher will start the procedure by engaging one of the ablest pupils in a model conversation in front of the class. Several may volunteer every day. The shy children should be encouraged to talk from their seats. The procedure of stimulating conversations between pupils continues throughout the years of foreign language study. The pupil should demonstrate that he has learned the structural patterns and his pronunciation should be acceptable. A grade is recorded according to his performance.

The following two examples of simple conversations are typical. All the discourse patterns will be reviewed as the teacher gives various pupils the opportunity to participate during the semester.

A. DANS UNE RUE FRANÇAISE
Bonjour, Monsieur Jacques.
Bonjour, Monsieur Pierre.
Comment allez-vous?
Très bien, merci, et vous?
Très bien, merci.
Voici une boîte pour vous.
Merci, Monsieur.
De rien.
Au revoir, Monsieur Jacques.
Au revoir, Monsieur Pierre.

B. EN CLASSE
Bonjour, Michèle.
Bonjour, Sylvie.
Comment vas-tu?
Très bien, merci. Et toi?
Très bien, merci.
Quel âge as-tu?
J'ai neuf ans. Quel âge as-tu?
J'ai neuf ans aussi.
Où est Georges?
Voilà Georges.
Au revoir, Michèle.
Au revoir, Sylvie.

TYPE 3: LIFE SITUATION

This kind of test demands a realistic statement of fact from the child. He must, therefore, in addition to performing the comprehension-response task, be able to change vocabulary items in his patterns to conform with the truth.

A. Quel jour est-ce aujourd'hui?
   Quel jour est-ce que-c'était hier?
   Combien de frères as-tu?
   Comment s'appelle ton père?

B. Each pupil obeys at least three commands given by the teacher, or another pupil, suiting the words to the actions.

Lève-toi, vas à la porte, ferme la porte, retourne à ta place.
Vas à la fenêtre, touche la fenêtre, frappe la fenêtre, assieds-toi.
Touche un livre, ouvre le livre, mets le livre sur la chaise.

TYPE 4: DRAWING TEST

One of the aims of nearly every test is to develop in the pupil the ability to understand and follow directions in the foreign language. Such is the purpose of the drawing test. It should be given without any special explanation if possible. The procedure is as follows:

1. Ecrivez votre nom sur le papier. Ecrivez le numéro 1, et dessinez une petite boîte. Ecrivez le numéro 2, et dessinez un livre.

2. Ten objects are drawn with pencil. The remainder of the list might include the following words: un *petit* chien, une *grande* fenêtre, un *gros* poisson, un *petit* chat, une *grosse* dinde, une étoile, un stylo, un *gros* crocodile.

3. Ouvrez le bureau, prenez la boîte de pastels, ouvrez la boîte, prenez le pastel noir.

4. The class is then told to color each object as directed, but the objects are not named in order and the number of each object is not mentioned.

5. The next day the graded papers are returned and discussed in French: Le numéro 1, qu'est-ce que c'est? Vas au tableau, dessine une petite boîte. One pupil complies. The teacher then asks: De quelle couleur est la petite boîte? Someone answers and all the questions are reviewed in this way.

The activities connected with this test are a practical application of material already learned. Children will enter into the spirit of the test and will find satisfaction in being able to follow directions in French. They will even worry in French like the boy who said: "*Mademoiselle, I don't have any jaune.*" or the one who said "*Mon chien isn't very good.*"

Another simple drawing lesson is an activity which may be considered a dictated test in the sense that the teacher can determine the amount of comprehension the pupils have developed. The teacher distributes sheets of paper upon which he has drawn a large head and neck. He then proceeds to ask the pupil to draw according to directions, for example:

Prenez tous vos crayons de couleur. Les cheveux sont châtains.
Les garçons, dessinez les cheveux d'un garçon. Les filles, dessinez les

cheveux d'une jeune fille. Dessinez les yeux marrons. La bouche est rouge et les dents sont blanches. Dessinez les oreilles noires. Dessinez le nez avec le jaune. Le cou est jaune.

The game *Es-tu artiste?* can be used to implement review work in the beginning of the second year. The teacher will conduct a review of colors, clothing, and parts of the body. He will then draw a large stick figure of a boy on the board or on an easel. Pupils may be asked to draw the features of his face, his shirt, trousers and shoes. The teacher will put a funny hat on him saying, *Oh, qu'il est drôle!* A picture of a girl is drawn in the same way.

Now the children are ready for a dictated drawing lesson which is a camouflaged test. These directions will be given:

> Nous allons dessiner un garçon. Il a les cheveux noirs. Il a les yeux marrons. Mettez un chapeau violet. Oh, qu'il est drôle! Mettez les crayons de couleur dans la boîte, fermez la boîte et mettez les boîtes dans les bureaux.

Riddles have also proved an effective means of testing comprehension; furthermore they make it necessary for some pupils to talk, especially those who present their own riddles to the class. Other activities listed under games may become informal testing devices in the hands of a skillful teacher.

ACTIONS TEST

The teacher displays a set of ten stick figures each one representing an action. Each illustration bears a number. The pupils letter their papers from "A" to "J" inclusive. The teacher states an action for each of the ten letters and the pupils write the number attached to that particular illustration beside the appropriate letter, for example, "Pour la lettre "A"—il saute," Beside letter "A" the pupils will write the number of the stick figure that is jumping. The secret of success in this test lies in large, bold, attractive stick figures and in being sure that the children understand what is expected of them.

INFORMAL STORY TEST

Culminating activities of a unit are sometimes evaluative. Pupils of an advanced class may be asked to draw pictures at home representing the activities of their respective families in the living room.

Each pupil shows his drawing to the group and describes what the various members of his family are doing. This challenging activity is an example of the correct use of creative ability. In a study of the house these pupils are perfectly capable of applying what they have learned to their own experiences. This work must be done orally: they are not asked to prepare a written story which they read or memorize. There should be no need for this—they are ready to communicate spontaneously.

In this case the teacher's primary aim in teaching a unit on the house has been to establish a number of basic discourse patterns in order to enable the children to talk about the activities of various members of the family. These discourse patterns may also lead to the presentation of a scene which is gradually developed through a series of drills and conversations.

In order to avoid any lost motion the teacher will bear in mind that learning the name of the rooms and articles of furniture, any notebook work which is done, the use of a doll house or discussion of language charts must all lead to the two culminating points, namely the description of the picture and the dramatization of the scene. These two activities are actually forms of evaluation.

GAMES AND EVALUATION

In this continuous process of evaluation which goes on in any good class, procedures other than drill may be employed. Games and contests are valuable activities which prepare the class for a test. A few examples to illustrate this point are the use of Bingo before a dictated numbers test; the contest entitled "Réglez l'horloge vite!" before testing the pupils' ability to tell time; and the questions asked by team captains before a comprehension test.

Quite often the same end, that of appraisal, may be achieved by having a pupil lead a game as by asking him to participate in a dialogue, since correct pronunciation, memory and several structural patterns are involved in both instances. From the teacher's point of view there is virtually no difference but there may be a tremendous difference in the eyes of the child who greatly prefers the excitement and the stimulus provided by the game. The game is more fun.

This does not mean that games should be overdone but this potent teaching device may be used wisely and it seems to have a legitimate place in testing on the elementary level. It would seem then, that there is sometimes a very fine line drawn between games and tests in FLES, as both provide the teacher with a means of evaluation.

USE OF THE TAPE RECORDER IN TESTING

There are various ways of using this valuable testing device in the elementary school: 1) Questions representing the basic structural patterns learned during the year are recorded on the tape by a native speaker. Commands, riddles, and stories may be included. While an assistant takes charge of the class, the teacher takes individual pupils out of the room and tests them. Each pupil listens to several questions and answers them while the teacher records a mark based on pronunciation and capacity for self-expression but the pupil's answers are not recorded. 2) If the teacher is obliged to administer this recorded test without assistance, the testing is done in the classroom and all the pupils hear all the questions and answers. 3) A blank tape may be used to record children's speaking ability. In this case individual pupils are tested out of the room. They are prompted by a question or directions given by the teacher, preferably in French; or the pupil may be asked to talk about a picture, a chart or set of pictures. His answers are recorded on tape. 4) Individual pupils may be tested in the classroom with everyone listening. This system requires a greater variety of subject matter to be tested and presents the problem of holding the interest of the rest of the class over a long period of time.

The use of a question tape in the classroom without an assistant has the advantage that the teacher is not required to spend long hours of listening to pupils' recorded answers after school. The following procedure is used in testing with the tape: first, a general review is conducted all in French using questions similar but not identical to those found on the tape. This preparation is not only important but necessary. Second, the question tape is presented in the form of an interesting challenge which the pupils readily accept. The children enjoy this activity if they are permitted to volunteer in an informal way. The teacher suggests that they try to answer as many questions as possible. Thus the stiffness of a formal test is avoided. Because the setting resembles that of a normal teaching situation there is very little tension. A clear explanation in the beginning is essential. Pupils must understand that they should volunteer for at least three questions; if they do not respond, they will be called upon. Experience has shown that this procedure produced results that were far superior to those obtained in the more formal situation when each child was called upon in a prearranged order.

This test is subjective in a sense but the objective testing of the speaking ability of a large number of children cannot be done thoroughly on this level with the means available. However, it can be done more effectively in the language laboratory of the secondary school. By the time the pupils have reached ninth or tenth grade they will have done so much oral work and they will have been subjected to so many experiences similar to the one just described that taking a formal, objective test should not be an ordeal for them. They will have developed quite a bit of self-confidence.

The results of the use of these tapes have been very satisfying. The pupils have an opportunity to hear and answer questions asked by a Frenchman, and above all they are being tested on material *they have learned*. The question tape offers a different kind of challenge to the pupils. The teacher may do a small amount of remedial teaching while the class is listening to the native voice, if this is necessary. He can help the class overcome any deaf spots; sometimes they need to be told to listen for a difference such as *la fenêtre* and *les fenêtres*. If a sentence is unintelligible to a class, the teacher should avoid repeating or interpreting it to the class unless it is absolutely necessary because this nullifies the advantage of having the tape made by a native speaker. He may find it necessary to play that part several times or give them a clue in French, for isolated questions out of context are harder to answer than those which are directly related to each other or to a specific subject.

Tape recorded questions that faithfully represent the teaching emphases of the course have proved to be an excellent testing tool. They provide the teacher with a means of checking class progress by evaluating achievement in terms of the pronunciation, intonation, and fluency of the individual members of the class. Such testing normally takes at least three days.

SUMMARY

English may be used if necessary in giving any of these tests for the first time. Using English eases the tension. When a similar test is given later, French may be used because the procedure is no longer unknown and feared. The attitude of the children toward the test is more important than adherence to a rule. "The attitude of the student (whether native or foreign) toward the test is, of course, of fundamental importance. Tests are delicate instruments and are no better than the situation in which they are used." [3]

This type of testing provides the teacher with some practical ways of evaluating the progress of his classes. Furthermore these tests are not only a means of measuring ability at the present time; they prepare the way psychologically for more formal work on the secondary level. One of the results of testing is "the development of effective methods of thinking." [4]

Children will exert more and better effort to meet the challenge of a test and to justify themselves in an evaluation process. To demonstrate his achievement to others is a matter of prime delight and importance to a child. A good program rests upon evaluation without which there is no evidence of true growth or progress. This is true psychologically from the child's point of view and pedagogically from the teacher's point of view.

SPECIAL TESTING PROCEDURES FOR SIXTH GRADE

In order to avoid a confusing break at the end of sixth grade it seems advisable to consider sixth and seventh grades as the transition years regardless of the administrative units of the district (8—4 or 6—3—3 plan). Through a blending of methods, materials, and testing procedures, a steady and careful progression can be achieved that builds a firm foundation for the text or course used in the seventh grade. The integration of new and familiar material

---

[3] Frederick B. Agard and Harold B. Dunkel, *An Investigation of Second-Language Learning* (Boston: Ginn and Company, 1948), p 261.
[4] Ross, *op. cit.*, p. 106.

should be so thorough that it would be difficult for a pupil to tell just where the elementary work stopped and the secondary began. As previously stated, evaluation and grades have been part of the teaching process in the earlier years. This process continues in the sixth grade, but the standards are a little higher and some reading is involved. There may well be, furthermore, a certain pressure on the teacher who knows that at the end of sixth grade, he must be ready to help make the decision about the future foreign-language study of his pupils. He will be expected to give evidence of their language achievement both in an absolute fashion for the seventh grade teacher's use and in a relative fashion to indicate the two ends of the spectrum in his group.

Occasionally, in an overzealous effort to be objective, administrators have called in "outside examiners." This practice has certain merits perhaps, but in addition to being foreign to American elementary school testing procedures, it has certain other drawbacks which outweigh its advantages. An outsider is seldom completely familiar with the manual used with the children. An adult using a parallel pattern but not the one the child learned will sometimes only baffle the child. Extraneous vocabulary is not a major issue as long as it is not the key to a sentence. In an unfamiliar situation a change of voice or rhythm may produce stagefright in a normally outstandingly able child. In short, countless unknown factors may invalidate the results of such an examination and make the whole procedure unsatisfactory.

A simpler procedure which is both educationally and linguistically sound, producing results which can be judged even by an "outside judge," is that of encouraging the FLES teachers as a group to continue their review-testing program of the earlier years and to create together certain tests and standards for the sixth grade. While care should be taken not to make them overstringent, the sixth grade standards should be higher than previously and the results should produce an honest picture of achievement according to the aims and philosophy of the program.

The following examples of sixth grade tests may be helpful in creating others appropriate to the material being used.

    I. Tests of aural comprehension.

        A. The pupils write ten dictated numbers (no words) as a formal test. As a preparation pupils should have had previous experience in writing numbers dictated by the teacher and by pupil leaders.

B. To test the pupils' ability to tell time in French, the teacher will distribute half sheets of paper on which ten clocks without hands have been drawn. The pupils set these clocks according to the teacher's directions.

C. The teacher distributes a sheet with ten pictures. He then directs the children that as he reads a numbered sentence they are to put the appropriate number in the corner of a picture.

II. Comprehension and expression.

The teacher will give a command to an individual child who, in addition to accomplishing the action, will say what he is doing, for example: JEAN: Donne une addition à Robert. JEAN: Combien font cinq et six? ROBERT: Cinq et six font onze.

TEACHER: Prends un cahier. Ouvre le cahier et lis une question, etc.

III. Tests involving reading and writing.

A. The pupils will match simple pictures in the appropriate, numbered labels, as shown in Example of Test 3a.

B. As shown in Example of Test 3b, the pupils will finish each sentence at the bottom of the page by copying the appropriate one from the choices given above.

IV. Oral expression.

A. A pupil may be asked to lead the class in a game.

B. Several pupils may be asked to dramatize a scene.

For practical purposes it is suggested that the teacher not try to give a grade for this work to every pupil during the same week. As different pupils volunteer to lead games or participate in dialogues, the teacher may give them their "test grade." Pronunciation, control of speech patterns, and the degree of difficulty of the particular assignment should determine the grade given by the teacher.

The end of sixth grade also seems a very appropriate time to administer a taped test of some length incorporating all these various testing devices with which the children are familiar. The taped test may possibly have one new element, that is, putting testing and taped material together. The children will have already experienced hearing and using taped material; they will already be quite used to tests, but the mechanical inexorability of the tape recorder will provide a real challenge and is an evaluative instrument for which they should be ready at the end of sixth grade. Such a test should be created by the whole corps of FLES teachers, voiced by as many as practical, paced by mutual agreement, but administered by each individual teacher to his own group. Performance on such a test is

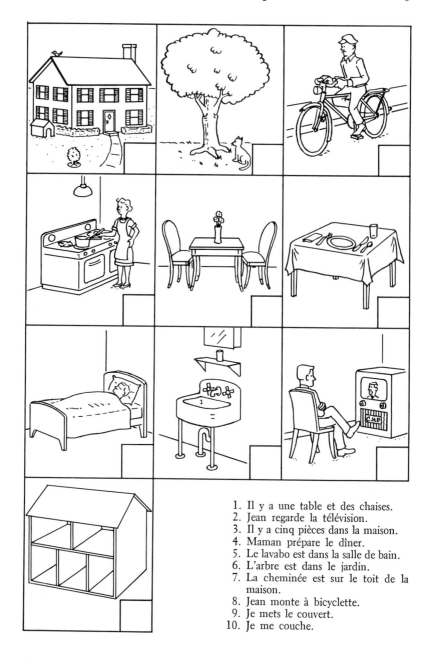

1. Il y a une table et des chaises.
2. Jean regarde la télévision.
3. Il y a cinq pièces dans la maison.
4. Maman prépare le dîner.
5. Le lavabo est dans la salle de bain.
6. L'arbre est dans le jardin.
7. La cheminée est sur le toit de la maison.
8. Jean monte à bicyclette.
9. Je mets le couvert.
10. Je me couche.

EXAMPLE OF TEST 3B

1. Comment vas-tu à l'école?
   Je vais à pied.
   Je marche.
2. Comment vas-tu au "Y"?
   Je vais à bicyclette.
3. Comment vas-tu en ville?
   Je vais en autobus.
   Je vais en auto.

4. Comment vas-tu à New York?
   Je vais par train.
5. Comment vas-tu de New York à Paris?
   Je vais par avion.
   Je vais par jet.
6. Comment vas-tu en France?
   Je vais par bateau.

Je vais _____

Je vais _____

Je vais _____

Je vais _____

Je vais _____

Je vais _____

not at all an absolute evidence of achievement or nonachievement, but it will certainly be of value to both the sixth and the seventh grade teachers in their task of screening the pupils.

HOW TO GRADE PUPILS

In one school system where French is taught three times a week, it was found most practical to give the pupils a mark for French at the end of each semester although pupils receive their reports four times a year. The teacher makes an honest effort to give every child the grade he seems to merit for a given amount of work. This grade represents the teacher's estimate of the child's progress in terms of A, B, or C. At least three marks are entered in the teacher's record book for every pupil by the end of the semester, for example, in fourth grade a mark is given for class work, one for an oral test, and one for conversation. From these three marks it is possible to obtain an average for the pupil report. In the second semester the three grades are given for classwork, a drawing test, and the year-end oral test consisting of questions recorded on tape.

As familiar work is reviewed in the fifth grade a mark may be given for specific work such as all the vocabulary and constructions related to clothing, another mark for the structural patterns related to giving and obeying commands, and another mark for spontaneous use of language. Participation in a dialogue about the house or in a restaurant scene, as well as the ability to discuss a language chart and respond to the question tape, are criteria for marking during the second semester. Thus at various intervals during the year pupils are aware that they are being judged upon their performance and that they are expected to demonstrate some fluency.

In the sixth grade written objective tests are given on numbers and time; at least two dialogues are learned; objective comprehension tests are given; a mark is given for accuracy and neatness in notebook work, for leadership as exhibited in taking charge of games, and for proficiency displayed in answering the questions on the question tape at the end of the year. On the pupil progress report the grades are marked as follows: an "A," "B," or "C" is given for French. The letter "S" indicating satisfactory progress, "I" is for improvement or "N" for need for improvement is shown for these two statements:

"Enjoys participation in French activities" and "Shows growth in oral-aural skills."

	GOOD	AVERAGE	POOR
Attention			
Comprehension			
Pronunciation			
Vocabulary Retention			
(might better be mastery of structural patterns or fluency or ability to use the language.)			

A more comprehensive report might include these items, levels to be indicated by the terms "above average, average, and fair."

	ABOVE AVERAGE	AVERAGE	FAIR
1. Pronunciation			
2. Attitude			
3. Comprehension			
4. Fluency			
5. Comments			

The teacher would consider these questions in marking the pupils. *Pronunciation* would include intonation and rhythm of speech. *Attitude* would have two interpretations, namely, he enjoys participation in all the activities of the French class, he has an open-minded, interested attitude toward learning a foreign language; it would also be interpreted as showing interest in the cultural aspects of the program. *Comprehension* would include ability to follow directions in the language, understanding demonstrated in comprehension tests such as the drawing test in fourth grade and the recognition of pictures in sixth grade, telling time and writing dictated numbers. *Fluency* would include vocabulary retention, mastery of structural patterns taught, ability to manipulate the language. Under *comments* the teacher has the opportunity to offer words of praise and encouragement, mentioning possible needs for improvement in certain areas. The teacher's personal interest in the child's progress can be an important motivating factor. Recommendations regarding future foreign language study would be included here, particularly at the end of the sixth grade.

Chapter VII

The Teaching of a Culture

The teaching of a culture was the subject of the 1960 Northeast Conference on the Teaching of Foreign Languages. According to the conference report:

> . . . . culture as it is used in this study refers to the sum total of the patterned manners, customs, norms, and values which are characteristic of a society. Language in this sense is inseparable from culture, and we as language teachers deal every day with a highly refined cultural phenomenon which we alone are equipped to discuss.[1]

Thus the FLES teacher's task is not solely to teach the correct forms but also to create the atmosphere in which American children can learn to use a foreign language; in the opinion of the writers of the Report it is impossible to teach the language successfully without making the pupils feel "at home in the culture."

---

[1] G. Reginald Bishop, Jr., ed., "Culture in Language Learning," *Northeast Conference on the Teaching of Foreign Languages 1960: Reports of the Working Committees* (New Brunswick, N. J.: Rutgers, The State University, 1960), p. 12.

There are many good ways of approaching the study of a foreign culture in connection with the study of a foreign language. Reading the lives of national heroes, men of science, or other notable people is one way; but there are several others. Various sections of a country have their particular geographical figures and their folklore, both of which may hold real interest for children. The juvenile literature of the country has possibilities: FLES pupils should be acquainted with at least one good story typical of the land whose culture they are studying. Foreign children's games, their school life, modern trends in their education, how they spend their free time are fascinating to American boys and girls. Older pupils like to study about such topics as chateaux, railroads, folk dances, and bull fighting. Indeed, FLES provides opportunity over a period of three or four years for the attainment of a depth of understanding of one ethnic group and its language, which could not possibly be achieved within the confines of the school's general social science curriculum. Whether the approach to culture and civilization be historical, geographic, scientific, literary, or a blending of these, it should accompany the study of the language from the beginning and throughout the entire FLES program.

UNDERSTANDING THROUGH PARTICIPATION

It goes without saying that the child's basic cultural experience in his FLES class is the foreign language itself. When he participates in his first conversation, he is introduced to the idea of shaking hands. The report cited above comments that even French hand-shaking is often accompanied by certain socially appropriate phrases and therefore belongs in the language classroom. The teacher must be prepared to teach such cultural patterns as these from the very first day. When a pupil says *J'ai neuf ans* or *J'ai faim*, he is participating in French culture; when he learns the correct use of *tu* and *vous* as two different ways of expressing "you" in French, he has again adopted a convention appropriate to the foreign culture. Culture and civilization are here understood to mean "people living, feeling, thinking, evaluating, acting"; therefore, teaching culture requires that the teacher devise ways in which pupils may "live," "feel," "think," "evaluate" and "act" so far as possible as do the foreign nationals whose ways they are studying.

PROVIDING A REALISTIC CLASSROOM ENVIRONMENT

To create a classroom environment that gives a feeling of realism with respect to a foreign culture requires of the teacher both imagination and initiative. The cooperation in various ways of a number of people is essential. One example of turning to an outsider for assistance would be arranging to have a foreign national visit the class. Pupils need the experience of meeting as many natives of the country they are studying as possible. The regular classroom teacher can be of considerable assistance if he is willing to help the students keep the FLES program in mind by pointing out references, displaying pictures, showing films and slides appropriate to the regular program that incidentally refer to or illustrate life in the foreign country. The music teacher can sometimes teach French songs without neglecting the regular program, perhaps tell the pupils stories about French composers if French is the foreign language being taught. The art department in many instances can provide suitable displays, encourage the illustration of French themes, even help in setting up an exhibit which will interest visitors. Physical education may do its part by teaching French folk dances. Parents of French—or Spanish, or Russian, or Portuguese—descent, if they are interested in FLES, may help in providing realia as well as by indicating their interest in and approval of the FLES program.

THE USE OF "REALIA"

Realia include slides, films, pictures, and above all *objects* actually used in the presentation of a given culture to students. The simplest materials are the best; realia should be easy to see, plain and uncluttered. When realia are at the focal point of a lesson, for instance, a film representing life in the Alps or slides of chateaux or of youth activities, they should be authentic and therefore a permanent part of the school's instructional equipment. However, this is not always necessary or practicable, in which case temporary expedients may be used as teaching aids or "props." If, for example, one is teaching a class the linguistic skills or discourse patterns necessary to set a table with an American setting, paper plates and paper silverware

are very practical as they can be put on a flannel board and easily seen by all. But a place setting of French china or at least one piece of such should be standard equipment for introducing the idea that France excels in the production of many luxury items.

IMPLICIT AND EXPLICIT METHODS

There are two possible approaches to the teaching of culture: in the first instance the culture is implicit in the teaching of the language. It is subordinated to the language patterns, for example: *C'est une maison française* is accompanied by showing a picture or model of a French house. This kind of teaching has a cultural impact. In a second instance the realia is the focal point of the lesson or unit and the teacher is explicitly teaching culture. Since the pupils' vocabulary is quite limited at best, some of this explicit teaching may be done in English. Pupils should be not only permitted but encouraged to ask questions; however, before they can ask intelligent questions they must be supplied with some facts and interesting ideas. The ensuing dialogues between teacher and pupils reach a high point of interest. A lesson of this sort, however, should not consume too large a percentage of FLES time, and may well be followed by a review session conducted wholly in the foreign language.

There are also two ways of using realia. One is to obtain authentic realia and adapt them to your teaching purposes. Realia at best are teaching aids and should be used mainly to create interest and never be permitted to become more important than the subject matter they are supposed to serve. Sometimes these teaching aids open the way for interesting correlations; for instance, an illustration of a Roman monument may inspire a pupil to do independent research on Roman architecture resulting in the drawing of a large arena. Or, in reverse, a story of mediaeval castles in the regular social science period may lead to a discussion of French castles resulting in a pupil-made model, thus enriching the pupils' concept of a particular period in history.

Another way to use realia is a unit center plan. In this the teacher or preferably the teacher and pupils together will select a center of interest and try to find illustrative materials. Holidays are a good example of this sort of plan. Lacking any authentic realia the FLES teacher may have a large picture of *Le Père Noël* copied from a French Christmas card. A series of large'pictures illustrating a French Christmas story can be painted with some directions and shown while the story is being told. Vocabulary should be carefully selected for this project, representing a good balance between old and new material. Whole sentences involving as many verbs as possible should be used and words not useful in any other situation kept at a minimum.

Another example of a center of interest plan is the ever popular unit on Paris, especially enjoyed by sixth graders. The unit is built around a filmstrip and models of several famous monuments.[2]

Realia skillfully introduced will encourage active role playing. Role playing properly done is one way in which American children may learn the viewpoints and mores of other cultures.

PLANNING THE COURSE OF STUDY

The teaching of culture is a continuous process from the first year of language study through the senior high school, and should never at any time be divorced from the actual learning of the language itself. On this there is general agreement among FLES authorities. But the basic question of organization remains to be answered for there is as yet no concensus on exactly what facets of culture should be taught in the elementary grades, which should be discussed in the junior high school, and what should be expected of the high school graduate in terms of intercultural understanding. Continuity of subject matter including provision for review is surely to be preferred to a haphazard teaching of cultural details; therefore, it is hoped that some measure of agreement as to grade placement can be reached by FLES teachers.

There is certainly agreement on the need for regarding the interests of the pupils as well as their several educational levels. The pupils will have sufficient time in the future to learn of the more adult facets of French civilization. The whole FLES program is a humanistic approach to language training; its aim is to produce students

---

[2] For a further description of this unit see the section on filmstrips in Chapter VIII.

capable of discussing the characteristics of a foreign culture in the language of that culture. We are trying to build an intelligent understanding of a foreign country, "rather than naïve good intentions that crumble the first time our cultural neighbor does something which is perfectly all right in his culture but strange or misleading in ours." [3] As we try to teach American children something of how French children live and learn, we know it is impossible to teach them everything and that it is better to teach a little and teach it well. In the elementary grades it is well to include only the most important holidays and those which appeal to children of this age; the celebration of St. Catherine's Day on November 25 holds no interest for these pupils, but they find *Poisson d'Avril* on April 1 (April Fools' Day) fascinating. A lesson on Gothic cathedrals is too academic for elementary school classes but will prove interesting to older pupils. When Paris is studied, the Eiffel Tower is a must, but l'Hôtel des Invalides should be saved for high school. Stories taken from the early history of France may be of interest to eighth graders who have acquired the necessary background but may confuse others who lack such preparation. The study of early French culture can be combined later with the study of ancient history. If the FLES teacher can provide good visual illustrations of Roman architecture, this would be one way of stimulating ambitious students to undertake individual research in this early period of French history.

The teaching of culture, especially in the case of younger pupils, centers on teaching the likenesses among the peoples of the earth. François gets up in the morning, eats the equivalent of an American breakfast, goes to school, comes home, does his homework, eats supper, goes to bed much as Jim does. But the differences among peoples must also be taught—we know our own country far better through comparing it with others. In making such a comparison, boys and girls should learn to withhold value judgments as to whether this French game is as much fun as a similar one played in our country, this particular action taken by a foreign teacher "right" or not, this particular prank "good" or not. The purpose is to help American pupils enter into the life of a foreign culture so far as is possible, to know about how their peers live and work in another

[3] Robert Lado, *Linguistics Across Cultures* (Ann Arbor, Mich.: University of Michigan Press, 1957), p. 8.

country so that they may begin to understand and be understood by people of other nations. With at least a modicum of understanding of the differences between two cultures, one may begin to learn to refrain from taking our own society as the sole norm by which other societies are judged and to avoid confusing the "different" with the meretricious.

The first step in the all-important process of learning to get along with others is taken in the home and the school environment. The second is taken when we begin to see other cultures as in some ways equal, in others less developed, in still others perhaps superior to our own.

Chapter VIII

Audio-Visual
Material & FLES

Audio-visual aids in FLES is a tremendously broad area; it ranges from the simple stick figure on the blackboard or colored magazine advertisements to full color TV presentation of material filmed in the foreign-language country. For this reason only certain principles and guidelines can be outlined in the space of one chapter. It is, moreover, important to establish at the beginning of such a discussion that such *aids* are *aids* to verbal communication and never an end in themselves. Even the most culturally accurate and meaningful object, filmstrip, or tape has little or no excuse for being in a FLES class if it does not elicit verbal reaction in the language of the culture it represents. By the same line of reasoning, a ludicrously awkward drawing which efficiently helps first to convey meaning and then to fix a pattern of communication is to be judged successful and worth preserving for re-use. Many FLES teachers, in a sincere effort to correlate either with art or some other elementary subject, have sometimes gotten language learning and audio-visual aids into reverse focus. This does not mean, however, that any teacher should not make every effort to have effective, attractive, and authentic aids or props for his teaching. It has been said that a FLES teacher is normally identifiable by the back seat of his automobile piled high with children's toys characteristic of a specific foreign country. For ease of discussion we shall separate aids to a teacher in a classroom quite distinctly from presentation over mass communication media such as radio and television.

OBJECTS AND PICTURES

Most FLES teachers have found by experience that teaching units beyond the classroom in scope, for example, the home or the family, can be greatly facilitated and enriched by model objects which the children can see and handle. A completely furnished doll house with a model family to inhabit it will facilitate teaching and create a kind of cultural bridge. Such direct association of an object with its foreign-language name avoids the interposition of the native tongue in the beginning and later may serve as the point of departure for "original" conversations. Furthermore, when the objects are authentic they are a spontaneous efficacious lesson in cultural differences and can also serve as the basis for linguistic drill. In such a context, it is well to remember that no civilization is completely represented by its folk art, however outstanding this art may be. By the same token, the child's tactile pleasure should not be inhibited by a museum piece.

Toys, such as a ball, jump rope, etc., will aid in teaching numbers by providing things to count in a real situation. Teachers have frequently found that language drill is not monotonous to the children where the props are varied and attractive to them. Many times a simple flannel board with attractive large (for easy viewing by the whole group) French magazine pictures stiffened by cardboard on the back will serve the purpose of presenting new linguistic material. These pictures may be of activities as well as of objects and once the patterns are mastered, children enjoy "creating" their own stories about such pictures.

LANGUAGE CHARTS

A more sophisticated but still relatively simple visual aid to teaching is the language chart. We have chosen to present several successful lessons developed from these charts.[1] Such visual aids provide the teacher with topics for discussion that are interesting to children and serve as a focal point for the attention of the class. The charts or pictures must be large, colorful, and uncluttered to be useful and should be easily visible from the back row. A considerable variety of activity is depicted in these scenes of life in France thus making it necessary to manipulate the language in describing the picture. The conversation will center upon the adults who appear to be working at various tasks and the children who are playing. The charts may be used in any grade including the eighth and provide an enjoyable way of reviewing elementary work for pupils in junior high school. Good charts present visual images which show to even the most casual observer a definite contrast to American scenes of a similar nature. Thus they are useful not only as subjects of conversation but also as pictorial representations of differences in culture.

Facility in speaking may be developed through the use of language charts. Just discussing the pictures is stimulating and interesting to the children even though they are not talking about themselves. The techniques which follow may be used with any chart but have proved particularly effective with the chart selected here.

STEP 1: INTRODUCTION OF CHART

An explanation may be useful when presenting the chart entitled *Le Jardin public* since the picture represents life in a large park in Paris. The teacher will mention that whole families usually go to this park together and that fathers often like to help the boys sail their boats. People of all ages enjoy the park; students go there to study,

---

[1] These charts—two of which are reproduced below courtesy of the publisher—are from André Michel, *Tableaux de vocabulaire*, and can be obtained from Fernand Nathan, Editeur, Paris.

and older people may spend the entire afternoon reading, knitting, or talking and watching their children. The fact that children of school age can go to the park only on Thursday or Sunday during the school year is an important cultural difference which should be noted. This brief introduction corresponds to the setting of the scene before teaching a dialogue.

It is understood that certain structural patterns that are basic to the course of study used in the school district should recur with every chart, for example, the methods employed in identifying nouns and the "What is he doing?" type of question, then the introduction of the pupil's personal opinion.

The presentation of this or any chart consists in a blending of the new material with what has been learned previously. New expressions are indicated by italics. Repetition by the entire group precedes individual repetition for practice. It is more fun to let the pupils volunteer for individual practice as everyone usually prefers to try his personal skill than to repeat by rows or other designated groups. Vocabulary previously acquired must be recalled; this may be accomplished by directing questions to various members of the class.

STEP 2: PRESENTATION OF CHART

A. Voici le *jardin public*. Il y a *beaucoup* d'enfants dans le jardin public. Est-ce qu'ils sont grands ou petits? Ils sont grands et petits. Regardez, il y a un bébé dans la voiture. La maman *pousse la voiture*. (To provide repetition of the new words, ask questions like *Que fait la maman?* One or two pupils may be asked to obey the following commands.) Montre une petite fille, un grand garçon, beaucoup d'enfants, le bébé dans la voiture, la mère, le jardin public.

B. Est-ce un cheval? Oui, c'est un cheval. Ce sont *les chevaux*. *Voici des chevaux de bois*. Le bureau est en bois. Le crayon est en bois. Je touche le bois. Les chevaux de bois *tournent*. Il y a aussi un lion. Que font les chevaux de bois? Les chevaux de bois tournent. Il y a de la musique. La jeune fille regarde les chevaux de bois. (Some practice is needed here. Now Parts A and B may be reviewed.)

C. Le cheval a une queue. La petite fille ici a une *queue de cheval* aussi. Je montre une petite fille blonde, une petite fille brune, et une petite fille rousse. (Practice.)

D. La petite fille rousse *saute à la corde*. La petite fille blonde joue à la balle. Le garçon joue avec le bateau. La jeune fille regarde les chevaux de bois. Que fait la petite fille blonde? etc.

LE JARDIN PUBLIC

Tableau de Vocabulaire d'André Michel. Reproduced courtesy of Fernand Nathan Editeur.

E. Qu'est-ce que c'est?
C'est une corde, une voiture, une balle, un cheval, un bateau, un ballon. Ce sont des ballons, des enfants, des chevaux de bois. (Children are familiar with the expression "ce sont" followed by "les" or "des.") Combien y a-t-il de ballons? De quelle couleur sont les ballons? Regardez la marchande de ballons. Une petite fille achète un ballon.

F. C'est jeudi sur le tableau. En Amérique les enfants sont en classe jeudi. En France les enfants *ne sont pas* en classe le jeudi. Ils sont dans le jardin public. Tout le monde *s'amuse*. En France les enfants sont en classe, lundi, mardi, mercredi, vendredi, et samedi.

STEP 3: THREE TYPES OF QUESTIONS

In this part of the lesson three types of response should be expected in the manipulation of the language: noun identification, description of actions, and the expression of abstract ideas. As soon as the pupils have assimilated the new material, the teacher may conduct a review in the form of a contest or he may call for pupil leaders to ask some of the questions. Prompting may be necessary. He will begin with *Qui veut prendre ma place?* Sample questions follow.

G. 1. Montre le lion, le garçon qui joue avec le bateau.
   2. Est-ce une petite fille brune? Non, ce n'est pas une petite fille brune. C'est une petite fille rousse.
   3. Montre beaucoup d'enfants, beaucoup d'arbres, beaucoup de ballons.
   4. Que fait le garçon? Que font les chevaux de bois?
   5. Qu'est-ce qu'il y a dans la voiture?
   6. Quel jour est-ce sur le tableau? C'est jeudi ou dimanche.
   7. Où sont les enfants français le samedi?

STEP 4: CLASS RELATES ENTIRE STORY

As the teacher or a pupil points to the various people in the picture the whole class says the sentences it has learned for them. A more coherent story will be obtained if related sentences follow each other. There is no need for simple identification of nouns as they served only as a point of departure during the presentation.

STEP 5: PUPILS VOLUNTEER ORIGINAL STATEMENTS

Another chart has been selected to illustrate this step because it affords many possibilities for pupils to express themselves creatively; this chart may be used effectively later in the second year.

Essential differences between French and American farms should be apparent from the chart, *La Cour de ferme*, one of these being the fact that the house and all the farm buildings form a kind of courtyard. The pupils may be told that most French farms are small, similar to this one, as opposed to the many large farms in this country. Wheat farms in central France might be compared to the farms of our Middle West. The filmstrip of a French farm further reinforces these observations and presents a true picture of everyday life on a farm in France.

A discussion of the chart is developed in French by describing the clothing and activities of the people in the scene, identifying the animals, discussing objects and parts of the house, making statements involving the use of the plural with the emphasis on *les* and expressions like *ce sont des pigeons*, and designating the location of objects on the chart such as *à gauche en haut de l'image* and *à droite en bas de l'image*. Several class periods will be required for a class to be able to talk about this chart successfully. The same techniques will be used. Variety and a change of pace will keep this study from becoming tiring.

STEP 6: DISGUISED REVIEW

To test comprehension and manipulation of the language the following procedure has proved highly satisfactory. The pupils, four at a time, approach the chart. Each chooses an item for explanation, identifies it, and gives his explanation to the class in sentence form. The children are eager to participate, actually vieing with each other to express themselves. The following are some of the statements made by the pupils during this procedure:

> Un tracteur tire la voiture rouge.
> Un cheval brun tire la voiture.
> Il y a des pigeons sur la tour.
> Ce sont des coqs.
> La vache donne du lait.
> C'est un petit camion vert et noir.
> La tour est grise.
> Les volets sont bleus.
> Le garçon a une chemise rouge.
> Voilà un tracteur rouge sur la route.
> C'est un petit chien brun.
> Un chien brun garde la cour de la ferme.

LA COUR DE FERME

Tableau de Vocabulaire d'André Michel. Reproduced courtesy of Fernand Nathan Editeur.

C'est une petite maison verte.
Voici un gros cheval marron.
Voilà un chien brun dans la petite maison verte. Il garde la ferme.
La grande maison est bleue, blanche, et orange.

Any chart is always good for quick recall and review. The chart
picture provides a stimulus or subject-matter for a conversation that
the teacher may channel by his introductory questions or remarks.
As the pupils become more familiar with any given chart, pupil
leaders may be allowed to take over the class and direct the conversation. The charts may also be used in the sixth grade as the basis for
reading known material. In this case the teacher needs only to put
together in narrative form the patterns the children have previously
used to describe or discuss the activities in the picture. He may then
give the children the story to "read." They read after the teacher at
first, then as self-confidence is gained, individual pupils eagerly volunteer to read aloud. The questions are answered orally before the
answers are written. In the following example of a reading lesson, the
chart in Step 1 is used in order to show how such charts can be uti-
lized at different levels and to demonstrate the principle of combining
new material with familiar or review patterns.

LE JARDIN PUBLIC

Il y a beaucoup d'enfants dans le jardin public. Une petite fille
rousse saute à la corde. Une petite fille blonde joue à la balle. Un
garçon joue avec le bateau.
Les chevaux de bois tournent. Une jeune fille regarde les chevaux
de bois. La maman pousse la voiture. Il y a un bébé dans la voiture.
C'est jeudi et tout le monde s'amuse.

1. Qui joue avec le bateau?. . . . .
2. Que fait la maman?. . . . .
3. Que fait la petite fille blonde? Elle . . . .
4. Quel jour est-ce? C'est . . . .

This technique may be applied to any subject matter previously
learned. It should be remembered, however, that reading is not the
primary aim of foreign-language teaching in the sixth grade. It is used
only to reinforce the oral skills during this important period of transition.

FILMSTRIPS AND SLIDES

In addition to the teaching aids just discussed, attractive and useful colored slides and filmstrips suitable for elementary French pupils are now available. Their greatest value lies in supplementing material in a given unit. Thus a study of the farm taught from the language charts *La Cour de ferme* and *Les Travaux des champs* is enhanced by a filmstrip that shows actual scenes of farm animals and buildings as they look at the present time. The language chart is a good visual aid for teaching, but the filmstrip with its series of pictures is even more effective in giving pupils an understanding of modern living in France and overcoming any feeling of strangeness toward the culture.

Suggestions for the use of slides and filmstrips in elementary school would include:

1. Preview the slides or filmstrip, and plan very carefully the language that you will use in the presentation.
2. Teach the lessons that prepare pupils for the slides or filmstrip.
3. Be sure you have mastered the physical aspects of showing the pictures.
4. Conduct a discussion after the showing in order to get the maximum amount of value from the showing.

This procedure is of some importance lest the slides or filmstrip become merely a travelogue or a form of entertainment rather than a teaching device. The wise teacher will not try to teach all of France in one year but will focus the attention of the class upon one region or one subject.

Many visual aids may be used in presenting a unit on a city or region in France: pictures, realia obtained in France, models of the Eiffel Tower or a Paris bus, even a Métro map, or a cultural television program. To bring all this to life and give the children a sense of really knowing the region or city, slides or a filmstrip or a movie can be of real value. A filmstrip on Paris can make the city very real to the pupils.

While the filmstrip is being shown, pupils hear new expressions in a lifelike situation. They have the opportunity to assimilate some expressions which are not actually taught such as *La machine met le lait en bouteilles.* They automatically assimilate expressions such as *beaucoup de circulation;* they are able to read the answers to questions about the typewritten story and to manipulate the language so that they can answer: *Paris est la capitale de la France.* They can also readily see a connection between *pieds* and *les piétons;* they can distinguish between *Qu'est-ce que les piétons?* and *Que font les piétons?* supplying *Les piétons sont des personnes qui marchent* for the first and *Les piétons marchent* for the second. All this material is well within the ability of the pupils; they have control of the structures used, understand the subject matter, can read it, and can help to give the commentary at the second showing of the film.

THE USE OF TELEVISION OR RADIO IN FLES PROGRAMS

FLES has proved to be a popular ground for experimentation in television teaching. There is something paradoxical in the idea of teaching an essentially active skill through a medium which provides motivation for activity but is powerless to control its quality or direction. Children under twelve would seem to have even less chance of success in learning through this medium than adults; it is even conceivable that pupils could learn wrong pronunciations as easily as correct ones. In spite of these serious shortcomings, many carefully planned television programs are now being conducted as educational research projects throughout the United States. In this chapter no effort will be made to debate the question of whether we should teach by television, since it is still too early to make fair and objective evaluations. Here we are concerned only with outlining certain basic principles and procedures, should it be decided to select television as an instructional method.

Most of the well-known television FLES programs are presentational programs, that is, the television is used either as the sole or as the first medium for presenting the language patterns and situations. There can be no doubt that with a master teacher with native or near native command of the language being taught, the presentation cannot fail to be impressive. Normally, however, some sort of reinforcement teaching is done either by traveling specialists or by the regular classroom teacher. In the first situation, the program budget must be generous; in the second, some sort of an in-service program for classroom teachers is essential. Some programs have successfully combined these last two approaches using specialist teachers as traveling resource teachers to aid the classroom teacher and to coordinate the program.[2]

Whatever the organization of the foreign-language television program, the most important step is a period of explanation and orientation with the regular classroom teachers. Whether the grade teacher is expected to participate in the actual program or is explicitly excluded from it, he can, as one person has expressed it, communicate to the children his opinion of the value of the program by the way in which he turns the television receiver on and off.

Compulsory participation on the part of regular grade teachers whether by administrative order or by social pressure seems unjustifiable from the foreign-language point of view as well as that of human relations. The classroom teacher cannot be "required" to supplement a master television teacher. Not all adults learn languages easily; indeed the very facts which justify foreign-language study for children under twelve may make adult foreign-language learning painful or even impossible to some excellent elementary teachers.

A good orientation program before the inception of the general program may eliminate many problems; it should consist of a full explanation and discussion with the principals, teachers, and any other staff members who may be concerned with the FLES project. The program, its aims, the educational philosophy behind it, and the specific requirements of any television teaching should be made intelligible to everyone involved. The importance to the success of the undertaking represented by each person's contribution to the plan should be fully discussed. Suggestions should be requested honestly and if possible volunteers recruited for an in-service training program. The higher the general interest engendered, the greater the chance of a real integration of the program into the life of the school and consequently into the total education of the pupils.

Quite often an in-service training program is telecast weekly for teachers in large metropolitan areas. Plans for the week's work are explained and techniques and procedures to be followed after the children's broadcast are described. This kind of program fulfills the

---

[2] For a full, carefully designed program of this sort, see the materials and reports of the Modern Language Project, 9 Newberry Street, Boston 16, Massachusetts.

functions of a course in methods and obviates the necessity for teachers to travel great distances for professional improvement. Foreign-language lessons taught over an open circuit also provide a form of adult education. Putting copies of the television schedule into the hands of parents in advance of showings offers an excellent opportunity to bring the public closer to the schools.

There are many varieties of television programs, each one designed to fit the particular needs and resources of the community. A successful program is built upon these blocks: a good model of authentic pronunciation, the pleasant personality of an interested television teacher, some form of live "follow-up" drill with the children, the cooperation of the entire staff and a total integration with the foreign-language teaching in the schools.

Although television teaching was not readily acceptable in its earlier stages, it has gained greatly in popularity during the last few years. When the screen is used as the sole means of presenting new material as in the Heath de Rochemont Program it has proved to be an effective aid to a classroom-oriented program. Whether the purpose of a particular program is to present the authentic pronunciation of a native speaker or to introduce a foreign culture, it is an extension of teaching power, since it brings to the classroom the concerted efforts of a team of experts. Television in this setting cannot be considered merely an "audio-visual aid," even though a large number of children can be taught and the barriers of distance overcome through its means.

The teaching of a culture is a phase of language teaching that can be well served by television. In the building of the program one teacher can do all the research on the culture, present his well-developed cultural lessons in English, and leave the rest of the staff free to teach the foreign language. Naturally, careful coordination between the telecasts and the work in the classroom is important. The number of subjects which can be discussed on a cultural background program is limited only by the number of facets of the foreign civilization which are interesting to children. The following list includes many possible areas of interest: geographical features of the country; winter sports and the Alps; Paris and Marseilles, a province and a small town; folklore and provincial costumes; dancing and local festivals; ways of observing Christmas, Easter, and birthdays; differences between other American holidays and those of France; the markets; meals at home and in a restaurant; houses; family life; what is done on Sunday; sports; schools in France and the attitude of parents and children toward school; chateaux and historical figures; scientists; farming; and contemporary life in France. Telecasts of this type are usually presented as enrichment, as a means of deepening the children's interest, or as cultural background necessary for an intelligent study of the foreign language.

The television teacher should be a master teacher—a highly skilled individual with plenty of resourcefulness who can operate under pressure. He must enjoy his work and have some conception of the possibilities of television as a teaching medium. Good video and audio reception in the classroom are essential. A blurred or indistinct picture or glare from windows can detract seriously from the learning experience. The teacher responsible for the individual classroom must understand that children in the back of the room cannot see small objects and pictures as well as those in front and act accordingly.[3] He must also realize that preparatory experiences, pupil participation in the lesson, and intelligent follow-up are needed if the pupils are to profit fully from their viewing.

Active rather than passive viewing is an important concept in educational television, as programs are carefully designed to conform to the age level interests of the children but not to entertain them. One means of holding the interest of the viewers is to ask them to participate in the broadcast by answering questions, repeating structural patterns, and singing. Various classes can be invited by the television teacher to cooperate in presenting a program. In this way pupils see and hear their peers in action, and a feeling of togetherness is obtained through viewing.

Questions for independent research should be offered by the television teacher at times. These suggestions may take the form of looking up information, building something, or preparing a skit. Individual projects of this nature should be strongly encouraged as it is only by doing independent research, by putting forth a real effort, using his own creative ability and intelligence that the pupil will experience any appreciative advance in his total education. Pupils frequently work on committees thereby gaining motivation from an exchange of ideas with their classmates and from seeking informa-

---

[3] No more than fifty children should view a program shown over a twenty-one inch screen.

tion from friends outside of school. Their need to find answers to certain questions that they have set for themselves or that the teacher has suggested acts as an excellent motivator.

Foreign language is also taught by radio in some school systems. In the absence of television or traveling specialists, instruction by radio has proved effective. In some cases such a program is considered enrichment or, in a sense, exploratory before foreign language is attempted in junior high school. In one case that follows the general pattern quite well, a series of fifteen-minute lessons once or twice weekly is planned for each semester. Usually every lesson is broadcast twice to allow the teacher to fit it into the daily schedule. Participation in the program is voluntary since wholehearted cooperation on the part of the teachers and students is needed. "Together they make the decision to study a foreign language and choose the language they wish to learn. The enthusiastic classroom teacher is the key to a successful program for only such a teacher can generate interest and develop proficiency among the pupils."[4] Under this system the entire class learns together.

The material taught is similar to that of any course of study; oral drill on basic structural patterns makes up most of the lesson. The teachers are also provided with manuals containing drills, techniques, and games. They are offered as much in-service training as time will allow. The extra time spent on foreign-language learning varies in every case but it is considered that the average time spent beyond the broadcasts is forty-five minutes a week.

Looking ahead for a moment, it seems realistic to predict that radio language programs will evolve more in the direction of supplemental programed material on a citywide or countywide basis rather than as the initial presentation of the language. Such radio material could be invaluable to stimulate new interest and effort among the children, to present their linguistic patterns in new contexts, and even to serve as informal tests of aural comprehension, as well as to provide cultural material of general interest that cannot be incorporated into the regular FLES course of study. Most school systems these days are equipped with effective radio communication facilities that might well be used to enrich the program of the FLES specialist.

---

[4] Leona Glenn, "Teaching Foreign Language by Radio," *Educational Research Bulletin*, Vol. XL, No. 5 (1961), 116.

Chapter IX

Administration: Planning,
Organization & Articulation

PLANNING AND ORGANIZATION

During the past fifteen years a significant evolution took place in the area of organization and administration of FLES programs. In the first enthusiastic surge after World War II, the only important point seemed to be to start a program and then later to worry about its nature and maintenance. Experience has taught everyone concerned that many problems can be avoided by careful planning before the inception of the program and even, that no program at all is preferable to one badly organized, taught by inadequately trained personnel, and leading nowhere.[1] Furthermore as FLES assumes its mature position as an integral part of the elementary school curriculum, the preplanning can more easily and effectively be handled by school administrators well acquainted with the practical problems of budget, allotment of time, the type of program best suited to the community, and other related problems. They can,

---

[1] See Appendix 4.

moreover, investigate thoroughly teacher needs and availability and plan orientation workshops for general elementary teachers as well as for the secondary foreign-language teachers. Paul M. Glaude, Foreign Language Supervisor for the State of New York, described such a committee: "It [the program] is established only after a careful, objective study of all problems connected therewith by a committee composed of administrators, foreign-language teachers, elementary school classroom teachers, and lay representatives of the community. . . ."[2]

Such a committee, once established, has before it questions to be resolved in three major areas: (1) orientation and communication, (2) overall policy decisions, (3) practical implementation of the program outlined as a result of the studies in the first and second areas. For clarity, the following discussion will be divided into these three parts although they are so completely interlocked that the separation is specious.

ORIENTATION AND COMMUNICATION

Many of the early FLES programs were first inspired by parent or other community organizations with the result that planning committees often included in their membership representatives of such groups as well as school administrators and language specialists. Within recent years, however, the pattern seems to have evolved to the point that, while such groups may be represented by official observers acting as liaison people to ensure adequate and proper communication of the policies formed, the official decisions are left in the hands of those officers already invested with the responsibility for school policy. The basic questions of which language or languages shall be chosen; whether the program shall be for all children in the elementary grades or a selected group; and if the latter, on what basis the selection shall be made, are all questions capable of engendering a great deal of unnecessary heat unless adequate explanation and orientation have been given. It still seems wise, therefore, to make positive arrangements from the very beginning for community orientation in this area. If the inclusion of laymen as members or observers of the planning committee is unfeasible, several open meetings for

---

[2] Paul M. Glaude, "The Establishment of FLES Programs," *Modern Language Journal*, (April, 1960), 158.

explanations and questions will greatly aid the enthusiastic acceptance of the official program.

In addition to community orientation, the active participation in planning by general elementary teachers as well as administrators and the secondary foreign-language teachers is eminently desirable because these two groups will be most affected by such a program. For the elementary school teacher it is not merely a question of giving up twenty minutes of precious time each day. He will, by his own attitude even tacit, communicate to the children a receptive or a negative attitude. It will be the classroom teacher moreover, who will be called upon in the final analysis to work out the details of correlation between the foreign language and the general curriculum. His enthusiasm for posters or other visual aids can promote or hinder the unconscious learning process. In short, the perceptive cooperation of each individual classroom teacher is vital to any FLES program, and time expended in explanation, discussion, and practical planning on the individual level is an important integral part of the preplanning phase of a FLES program. During this period some thought should be given also to the organization of a permanent liaison committee between the FLES teachers and the general elementary group to explore and plan together new areas of mutual interest as the program evolves.

The secondary foreign-language teachers also need to be active from the very beginning of any discussion of a FLES program. At some stated moment, two or four years hence, this group will be asked (or forced) to change its entire curriculum, to adjust to a group of youngsters who have already had experience with a foreign language and possess some degree of skill in using it. The reaction to such a new situation has generally been one of pleasure and enthusiasm. Occasionally however, it has been characterized by fright resulting from insecurity. One teacher was once heard to exclaim: "But what ever will become of eighth grade French?" The new methodology of audio-lingual teaching may also make uneasy some teachers committed wholly to the grammar-translation method and hence, by lack of practice, less fluent in the spoken language than the children coming from the FLES program. These problems are extreme examples and not too commonly found of course, but even the master teacher in the secondary schools will have to plan a completely new curriculum based on the new program. Furthermore, at the planning stage, the secondary foreign-language representative will probably be the only foreign-language specialist on the committee. His word should carry much weight in the technical problems of program articulation and continuity.

The administrative body will need representation from both the supervisory personnel and the principals. Among the latter, principals of junior high schools are as important as elementary principals, for in addition to the general philosophy and policy affecting the children under their direction, these principals will be charged with working out the physical details: time schedules, room arrangements, teacher loads, etc., for their schools. Since even in large school systems, the FLES teacher possibly may not spend a whole day in one building, the administrative officer needs to have an overall view to help him make efficient realistic arrangements.

There is much to be gained if each of these representatives acting as a liaison person be explicitly charged with reporting to his group the discussions and decision of the committee and reporting to the committee the reactions and suggestions of his group. Active involvement of all of the groups will ensure acceptable democratic decisions and lead to the healthy cooperation so vital to any FLES program. Such a procedure may require a great deal more time (a year to eighteen months seems to be the norm), but the results will in a very concrete way spell the success or failure of the undertaking.

POLICY DECISIONS

The vital factors in overall policy decisions on FLES have been clearly and cogently outlined by a national group of FLES specialists at a meeting called by the Modern Language Association in January, 1961. Their statement read in part:

> A FLES program should be instituted only if: 1) it is an integral and serious part of the school day; 2) it is an integral and serious part of the total foreign-language program in the school system; 3) there is close articulation with later foreign-language learning; 4) there are available FL specialists or elementary school teachers with adequate command of the foreign language; 5) there is a planned syllabus and a sequence of appropriate teaching materials; 6) the program has the support of the administration; 7) the high school teachers of foreign language in the local school system recognize the same long-range

objectives and practice some of the same teaching techniques as the FLES teachers.[3]

The strength of this policy statement lies in its unequivocal commitment on certain practices which until that moment had been diverse to say the least and which in many instances had only confused the public and precluded any clear definition of such an educational program. Successful deviation continues to exist on individual points, but it is quite fair to say that this statement represents the unanimous consensus of leaders in the field. There can be no doubt about the value of the statement as a starting point for discussion of any new program. Using this statement then as basic policy, other decisions peculiar to the particular school system need to be made.

First, the important decision between a program for *all* youngsters or one for a selected group must be made. The total program is designed to provide to every child of elementary school age some experience with a foreign language at the optimum age for learning and to give each child, in addition to linguistic skill and cultural knowledge, more receptive and open attitudes toward civilizations and languages other than his own. Such a program will inevitably, to a certain degree at least, bring a secondary but not unimportant result: the relatively easy selection of children with special aptitude and interest for foreign language who should be encouraged to develop this capacity. Concomitantly, it will also help provide more information about children who, because of psychological block, aural problems, or sheer lack of interest may not profit from further insistence on foreign-language learning.

The disadvantages of a total program are quite simply told: first, there are more children to be taught, hence, the budget must be larger and the special teachers more numerous; second, the program must be planned for the average student rather than for the gifted child. This last certainly does *not* mean that the program is any less valid or does less well what it sets out to do, but merely that it would be wrong to subject an average child in a class of thirty-five to the same material and evaluation standards as those used for a group of fifteen to twenty gifted children.

---

[3] Donald D. Walsh, Introduction to "A Survey of FLES Practices" by Nancy V. Alkonis and Mary A. Brophy as quoted in *Reports of Surveys and Studies in the Teaching of Modern Foreign Languages 1959–1961* (New York: Modern Language Association of America, 1961), p 213.

The selective program, on the other hand, can provide a challenging high level of linguistic skill and cultural knowledge at the child's point of mature understanding. The major problems in such a program are the adjustments to be made in the general elementary program for small groups of children and, even more directly, the basis for selection. Psychologists seem agreed that the correlation between intelligence and language learning "is not so high as to indicate that intelligence is the major factor in determining success or failure in language work."[4] Reliable prognostic tests for language learning are only presently being constructed so that until they are validated, there is no reliable objective prognosis.

The most cogent argument in favor of the total program rather than the selective one remains in the end, however, the conviction that adult contact with people of other languages and cultures is no longer an aristocratic experience for Americans. Soldiers, technicians, and professional people, not to mention tourists, go abroad by the millions each year now. This movement is more likely than not to increase as the world becomes more truly "one world." No one can predict accurately which foreign language will prove utilitarian to a particular individual, but it is generally accepted that each successive foreign language is learned with greater ease. The open attitude of acceptance of differences is not the least of the valid results of a sound FLES program for all children.

The question of which language is the second item that should be considered with great care. We have repeatedly stated in this book that any child beginning a foreign language in the elementary school must be assured the opportunity of continuing this language throughout his public educational experience. This principle is of utmost importance and may be the key to the choice of the language or languages taught. Even for a large metropolitan system it may prove too heavy a budgetary burden to introduce nine years of a new language. The most practical and intellectually sound principle seems rather to be to choose a language already taught in the secondary schools and to plan an adequate articulation program between the new program and the existing one. It is important to note, nevertheless, that no language with a written cultural history is *per se* any better than another and a careful consideration of the cultural back-

---

[4] Harold B. Dunkel, *Second-Language Learning* (Boston: Ginn & Company, 1948), p. 80.

ground of a given community may indicate a choice not commonly made to date in American comprehensive high schools, for example, Polish, Chinese, Portuguese, or Italian, where the cultural antecedents of the community warrant such a choice. In general, however, the choices will probably continue to be French, German, Russian, or Spanish. The Texas Foreign Language Association lists succinctly these factors in choosing the language to be introduced: "a) social significance or world importance of a language, b) cultural background of the community, c) availability of teachers, d) national interest, e) provision for continuity in junior and senior high school."[5]

Various communities have also tried offering some sort of choice or starting a number of languages in rotation by years. This latter method creates tremendous administrative problems: a junior high core of teachers in each language in rotation must be created and odd combinations of foreign-language experience is produced among various children in the same family. Holdovers pose a problem under this system, whereas if the same language is taught every year, a pupil who is repeating a grade can usually demonstrate some fluency in the language thereby increasing his self-confidence and improving his peer status. One community wanting to start three languages did so by arbitrarily assigning one specific language to each elementary building in the community. This arrangement provides an even flow in all three languages to the secondary level and assures the fact that all the children in a given family learn the same language. Of course there is no choice for the child and the question of transfers even within the same school system becomes a real problem.

The most practicable solution seems to be to build the FLES program on one language, or at most, a choice of two if the system and budget are large enough to support a choice. Where there is only one language taught, seventh grade or the beginning of junior high school should present the possibility of continuing the same language or changing to another for valid reasons. Special concern must be shown also to bring to the verbally gifted child some experience with a second foreign language and with an ancient language, probably Latin, during the secondary school experience.

A factor in the choice of any language, in addition to adequate continuity, must be the potential and actual supply of well-trained

---

[5] *Texas Foreign League Association Bulletin*, Vol. II, No. 2 (March, 1960).

teachers. Many FLES programs have been something less than ideal for want of teachers both highly skilled in oral language (models for the children) and well grounded in the methodology to be used in such teaching. There can be no question that the FLES teacher must be more than an adequate practitioner of the language and the art of teaching or disastrous results will break not only the FLES program itself, but the secondary language continuation.

During the first decade of the FLES movement many programs were begun on the basis that each classroom teacher would teach his own class the foreign language chosen. This hypothesis has proved to be highly impracticable. The elementary teacher already has as many duties as he can discharge adequately; some know no foreign language and are willing but unable in adult life to learn another language. Not all the teachers in a single building have had the same foreign language, and perhaps most ironically, many teachers studied foreign language in school and college but not as a means of audio-lingual communication. The result of these findings has been a marked move in the direction of specialist teachers with very real aid from willing and able elementary teachers who are in the process of becoming specialists through summer work or in-service language programs.

At least one state (Ohio) has certification as Foreign Language Specialist so that the same person may teach a given foreign language in any grade from one to twelve. This certification may be approached either from initial elementary certification by the addition of foreign-language subject matter certification or from a secondary foreign-language certification by the addition of courses in child development and in the principles of the elementary school.

When these major policy decisions (who? what? by whom?) have been thoroughly explored and decided, the same committee will probably be called upon to plan the implementation of their decisions. A variety of points of view is particularly necessary at this juncture to ensure the smooth running of a new program and organize the minimal adjustments necessary for efficacious handling.

IMPLEMENTATION OF THE POLICY

One of the first problems to be resolved in the actual implementation of a program is the appointment of a coordinator, that is, the teacher of the FLES corps who will take on the responsibilities of unifying and administering the program as well as planning the coordination with both the elementary curriculum and the secondary language program. One of the newer aspects of FLES has been the preference of the title "coordinator" rather than "supervisor," which has evolved perhaps by chance, but which underlines the cooperative spirit of teamwork rather than the inspection-from-above factor. This person should be experienced in FLES work, know the teaching materials, have organizational ability and, especially, tact in human relations. He must be allowed planning time both before the inception of the program and during its first years so that visitations, workshops and articulation meetings form an integral part of his professional work.

Many programs began with pilot classes and were enlarged by popular demand without adequate unity and planning authority, but this experience has proved quite generally the fundamental need for the official leadership of a person aware of the overall problems. The larger the corps of FLES teachers, the more vital the unification, since there is no written textbook. Either too much or too little imagination will cause problems at the point of transition to secondary language work. Coordination is essential to ensure that cultural and attitudinal aims are neither lost entirely nor overemphasized. Furthermore, as we have seen, the coordination both to the general elementary and to the secondary school language programs, not to mention the administrative aspect of time and space within a particular building, will require the expert advice of a person actively engaged in FLES teaching, working with these various other groups affected. Graphically the coordinator's position might look something like this:

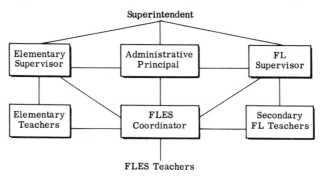

After the appointment of the coordinator, the specific decisions of implementation deserve the full attention of the planning committee. Some of the problems may not seem to merit discussion, while others are of fundamental importance, but in every case, a clear decision at the beginning will help smooth the inception of the program. At what grade should the program begin? How long should the class period be? How many times a week? Should foreign language be taught in a special room or in the regular classroom? With the classroom teacher present or not? How many classes can a FLES teacher teach per day? Is travel time involved?

Although at least one eminent authority on FLES has advocated starting as soon as possible, as early as the first grade,[6] the recent trend has tended to fix the ideal point for initiating a FLES program at grade three or grade four. The child then has a fair start toward mastery of reading and writing in his native language, and he will have a chance to develop such mastery while enjoying at least two years of audio-lingual training before he begins to read and write in the foreign language. The school budget is not infrequently the deciding factor in choosing the initial grade and rightly so, for continuity and articulation must take precedence over a very early beginning.

Similarly length of periods and the number of meetings a week are ideally set at twenty-minute to half-hour periods five times a week, although compromises to scheduling and budget sometimes lower this to three twenty-minute periods a week. Anything less than this minimal three twenty-minute periods a week is, in our opinion, risking too much effort and money on the child's facile memory. Quite often foreign language is taught for twenty minutes three times a week for the first years and the length of the period increased to twenty-five and thirty minutes in grades five and six respectively. In the junior high school, where there has not been a foreign-language program, the problem of finding time in the day sometimes proves to be more complex than it seems. There is once again no absolute pattern. One community offers foreign language for half the normal period five days a week in seventh and eighth grades and increasing to a full period in the ninth. Another plan is full regular periods from

---

[6] Theodore Andersson, *The Teaching of Foreign Languages in the Elementary School* (Boston: D. C. Heath & Company, 1953), p 11.

seventh grade through twelfth. A third possibility which has had some success is three periods a week in seventh and eighth grades with the regular five in ninth grade. Any compromise from the five full periods beginning in seventh grade is a compromise to the skill-habit formation nature of language learning and when the "exposure time" drops below three times a week, the validity of the program becomes questionable.

The question of a special classroom has found many advocates who point out that the child thus speaks only the foreign language in certain surroundings, that he learns to associate certain verbal patterns with those surroundings. Psychologically too, his loyalties are not divided between two teachers but go entirely in the direction of the foreign-language teacher who, in turn, is in complete command of the class while they are learning the foreign language. The teacher can create an atmosphere by realia and can act more independently.

Other FLES exponents believe equally strongly that the foreign language should be taught in the regular classroom so that any realia can be seen all day long, so that the classroom teacher can integrate the foreign-language learning into his other work more easily, so that the child does *not* isolate his foreign-language experience into one single atmosphere. Obviously in this arrangement the key lies in the mutual understanding, cooperation, and enthusiasm for the program that exists between the traveling teacher and the regular classroom teacher.

When a traveling specialist is used in a FLES program, scheduling can become a problem of intricate detail dependent entirely upon a realistic consideration of the local terrain (distance involved, travel time in winter, traffic conditions, one-way streets, parking, etc.). These may seem to be minor details, but upon them frequently depends the spirit of the teacher and hence the children. Once these details have been plannd for smooth operation, the actual teacher load must be considered.

FLES teaching, like any other special teaching (music, art), means that the teacher meets large numbers of children and must know each child individually. He must have time to consult their records, their classroom teacher, and their parents if desirable. Furthermore, since FLES teaching is completely active, it is intense for thirty minutes, sparked almost entirely by the teacher with no book to fall back on on an "off day." These factors have led administrators to conclude that a FLES teacher cannot teach more than nine to ten classes a day effectively on a five day schedule or fourteen to fifteen classes per week on a three day schedule. A ten minute "breather" in the morning will make the fifth class more enjoyable and allow the teacher to rethink his preparation. In fact, a few minutes are needed for making notes after each class. We are aware that nine to ten one-half hour classes do not fill the normal school day, but this schedule may mean that the teacher has actually taught from 250 to 400 different children during that time. It should also be remembered that the children cannot invent language in this class and that therefore the teacher is simultaneously responsible as model, critic, and teacher.

It is evident from all of the foregoing discussion that ideally and, in great measure, practically, the successful FLES program should be taught only by specialist teachers. Sometimes this is not possible, but compromises with this principle must be weighed in the light of the effect on the children of an inaccurate model or of a teacher lacking understanding of young children. An additional consideration is what effective means can be found and used immediately to bring the teacher's level of competence to the levels set forth by the Modern Language Association for all foreign-language teachers.[7]

We have not thus far spoken directly of budget though such considerations have been implied. The committee may want to apply the democratic concept of "the greatest good to the greatest number." On the other hand it will also have to consider the practical aspects of the question and is advised to adopt that plan which *the district can best afford with continuity, providing that well-qualified and effective teachers are an essential part of the plan.* Ideally it would be profitable to offer foreign-language study to all children at an early age. When this plan is financially impossible, it may be advisable to start with slightly older children.

While considering these questions, policy makers should remember that there is no given set of solutions. This discussion is intended merely to guide administrators and teachers as they plan and develop a program that suits their particular needs and that uses the resources of the community to the best possible advantage.

----

[7] See Appendix 3.

ARTICULATION

The past ten years of growth in FLES programs has provided much valuable experience at the extremely delicate and crucial point of the successful FLES program, namely, the point of articulation with the traditional program in the secondary schools. In many school systems no foreign language had been taught at the junior high school level before the FLES program began. Therefore, an entirely new curriculum had to be devised that would flow easily from the foreign language study in the elementary grades and progress to some sort of articulation with the ninth or tenth grade program, providing a modicum of flexibility to allow for individual counseling and guidance at two points in the pupil's academic development. The purely administrative problems of finding time in the junior high curriculum and finding able teachers to staff the new courses frequently obscured the necessity for allowing time to plan a sound curriculum articulation.

School systems having foreign-language courses beginning with the seventh grade were faced with an immense readjustment as youngsters who had already had experience in one of these languages entered the seventh grade. Latin teachers were startled to find that they no longer provided the first experience with a nonnative language. Administrative problems were at times compounded by the direct clash of methodology between the FLES teachers and traditionalist secondary school language teachers. It would be both inaccurate and ungrateful to the pioneers to minimize the problems of articulation. In city after city, successful results seem to have come only through the patient and tactful handling of human relations during this difficult period of adjustment. By now, however, administrative problems have been solved in enough systems to provide certain general guidelines. The NDEA Institutes have made the audio-lingual methodology less esoteric and frightening to many secondary school teachers, and in addition, such programs have perceptibly increased the actual language fluency of foreign-language teachers at all levels. The aims and methods of foreign-language teachers have also undergone an important psychological change in that elementary, secondary, and college level teachers no longer feel completely cut off from one another. The level is now viewed as a convenient division in the human psychology of learning—a division which influences the emphasis or approach to the four skills generally accepted as necessary to language learning, namely hearing, speaking, reading, writing.

All of this progress greatly simplifies the present situation but does not change the fundamental factor of the delicacy and importance of a careful articulation between the FLES program and the secondary schools. Furthermore, the essential factor will continue to be the tactful handling of human relations, based in large measure on adequate communication and planning. There are two main areas of articulation which for clarity we shall call 1) language curriculum and 2) general and administrative. Obviously this is an oversimplified picture, but it represents the two focal points of adjustment. Before taking up these individual points, it is appropriate to refer again to the Revised Policy Statement resulting from a conference of FLES specialists at the MLA in January, 1961:

> It required: 1) a foreign-language program in grades 7 and 8 for graduates of FLES, who should never be placed with beginners at any grade level; 2) a carefully planned coordination of the FLES and secondary-school programs; 3) a frequent interchange of visits and information among the foreign-language teachers at all levels; 4) an overall coordination by a single foreign-language supervisor or by a committee of administrators. These cooperative efforts should result in a common core of language learning that will make articulation smooth and effective.[8]

The articulation of the language curriculum is most easily handled in systems where there is a foreign-language supervisor who has the overall view and responsibility for foreign-language teaching at all levels. Under the leadership of such a person, unity of aims and methods is more easily attained. Furthermore, one person is already charged with the responsibility for coordination and has the means to call meetings of teachers from all levels of the language program for orientation and planning. Where such a supervisor does not exist, the superintendent may well feel the need to delegate this responsibility to an able leader among the foreign-language staff so that within a period of three to five years a smoothly articulated curricu-

---

[8] The Revised Policy Statement was the result of a conference held in January, 1961. It is reproduced in its entirety in Appendix 4.

lum flows from grades 3 to 12 with shorter or variant curricula from 7 to 12 or 10 to 12 for each of the foreign languages represented in the system.[9] These curricula should represent unity of aim and methods, continual advance in depth knowledge of the linguistic skill and culture represented by the foreign language, and practical measures for the maintenance of the skill and knowledge acquired at previous levels.

It is hardly necessary to point out that the definition of the unified aims and the participation at each level will be effectively attained only within the frame of reference of a particular system. We offer the following general guidelines, nevertheless, as a possible starting point for more concrete definition:

General Aims:

1. To develop in the youngsters a fair degree of skill in handling the four aspects of foreign language: hearing, speaking, reading, writing.
2. To develop an accurate, modern knowledge of the culture of the country including some introduction to its literature.

Such a program cannot be effectively accomplished if all segments are attempted simultaneously. Like a great system of rivers it should be comprised of tributaries and add to the original source, so that by the last years of senior high school, the general definition above should be discernible in the competence attained by the students. Specifically it might go somewhat in this fashion:

Grades 3 to 6.	Hearing and speaking everyday linguistic material representative of the culture in the anthropological definition. Pre-preparation for reading and writing.
Grades 7 to 9.	Hearing and speaking continued with the addition of reading and writing. Simple functional structure analysis. Cultural emphasis still basically anthropological but with some specific literary reading.
Grades 10 to 12.	Introduction to literature through the language as a tool. Composition and oral exposition emphasized from the linguistic point of view. Such remedial work in pronunciation and structure as is necessary to safeguard linguistic skill in handling the verbalization of sophisticated, personal thinking.

For the groups which begin at any point after the third grade the

---

[9] Nelson Brooks, *Language and Language Learning* (New York: Harcourt, Brace & World, Inc., 1960), p. 118.

progression will be much the same beginning always with hearing and speaking but not arriving at quite as sophisticated a level in the twelfth grade.

Unity of aim must be accomplished by essential unity of method and technique. This statement should in no way be construed as a rigid straitjacket put upon the individual teaching personality, but diversity is amply possible within the basic audio-lingual approach. For this reason it has seemed wise in many systems to have one committee representing all the levels choose the textbooks to be used at each level. Such decisions require general familiarity with the work and aims at each level and cognizance of the necessity for a continuum of vocabulary as well as structure. In such cases the committee procedure has led to healthy intervisitation among language teachers at the several levels thus creating a greater sense of teamwork toward a single goal.

It is not out of place to say a word here, in a book on FLES, about the junior high school course and teacher. The best teacher at this level is gifted with special flexibility—the talent for taking each group of seventh graders where he finds them and leading them to the point where the senior high school teacher would like to have them. Experience has shown that even a brief experience at the elementary level will give the junior high school teacher the practical familiarity with the materials and methods which enable him to judge very quickly the performance of a given group against the standards set by the FLES teachers. He can review patterns efficiently while he is also introducing new material. In cases where the elementary experience for the junior high teacher is not feasible, frequent meetings and observations can, in some measure, compensate.

The second group of problems termed "general or administrative" are not really very different from those encountered in other subject matter fields. While still exploratory in the junior high school, the curriculum becomes more limited and less general with increasing "extracurricular" demands on the child's time so that inevitably a process of choice becomes involved. It is evident that this process of choice requires clear criteria against which some concrete measurement can be set. In Chapter VI, we discussed sixth grade testing in a special category in an effort to provide concrete judgment of individual achievement. There remain however other factors to be considered by all those concerned with the individual child's decision.

Foreign-language teachers have not always been completely articulate in orienting and aiding the guidance staff in their counseling work. Within recent years, however, much progress has been made in clarifying to all sorts of educational groups the importance of continuity in foreign-language study as well as the increased rewards of knowing one language and culture well rather than merely touching several with no lasting result. Exploratory language courses are also less common than they once were because what seemed theoretically a good idea has in fact been difficult, if not impossible, to teach, has created false conclusions about language study and, according to some observers, has even tried to build the linguistic house from the roof down.

Within a potential nine-year sequence in foreign-language study there are at least two points when the aid of the school's guidance staff is of particular importance: at the seventh grade level and again at the tenth grade. Let us postulate a system where foreign-language study is begun as a total program (for all children) in the third grade. By the end of sixth grade, a careful screening is made, as we have seen, by the foreign-language teacher. Other factors would probably include: 1) interest and attitude 2) fluency demonstrated in class 3) at least average achievement in written English 4) general academic standing or the standardized test scores in basic subjects 5) the recommendation of the classroom teacher 6) parental consent. It is obvious that a consultation between the classroom teacher and the language teacher is necessary in order to arrive at the correct decision for each student because the factor of child growth and development enters into the question along with learning potential. The mechanics involved in this operation are important if the promotion from sixth grade to seventh grade French classes is to be accomplished easily. The result of the testing, the wish of the child, and the decision made in consultation by the teachers should be assembled into a recommendation that the child 1) continue his study of the *same* language 2) for some *valid* reason (such as cultural ties or parental pressure), continue his language study but in a new language 3) that the child discontinue his language training.

The counselor will quickly find that the first alternative is by far the most frequent and most consonant with modern foreign-language theory. The second alternative can only be "played by ear" since what is "valid" in one case is not in another. In light of present day foreign-language theory, this alternative should be the rarest of the three and reached only after quite thorough discussion of the factors entering into this decision to interrupt the continuity of the foreign language already begun. The third alternative will most frequently become apparent from the total record of scholastic achievement for an individual child: low achievement because of reading or hearing problems; emotional disturbance or immaturity resulting in difficulty in communication. There is even the child, normal in most ways, but belligerently antagonistic for some reason to his FLES experience. Given the high memory factor in foreign language study and the importance of attitude and will in such learning, a sincerely antagonistic attitude should result without question in withdrawal from foreign-language study.

The junior high counselors may also want to guide the verbally able child toward the study of Latin as well as his modern foreign language to widen his horizons historically in addition to the horizontal or international breadth gained from modern foreign language study. We have used the word "verbally able" to indicate a broader group of children than simply future linguistic specialists. The "verbally able" will include youngsters bound for the professions, those who communicate well with ease and pleasure, those who, in large measure, will be responsible for re-interpreting the occidental heritage to their generation.

At the end of the junior high school experience a second careful screening of these youngsters is necessary to determine who should be encouraged or cut off, who has future plans stable enough to indicate same change, who will want to add another modern language, etc. Another kind of screening may well take place at this point among the group which is continuing its foreign-language study. This screening should be based on sheer achievement (FLES and junior high starters)—ability to handle the four skills involved in foreign language learning. The very top performers should be urged to do Advanced Placement work in a special section in grades 10 to 12.

Occasionally a child will show no interest, even be antagonistic at the end of junior high school but "be required to have a foreign language to enter college." It might be suggested that where the system can arrange it, these students be released at the moment but given a "refresher" course in 12th grade to prepare them for placement and continuity in college. Counselors and foreign language teachers alike are all too frequently baffled and frustrated by negative attitudes toward requirements of higher education. Low achievement, resentment, and compounded negativism will result from insistence in the foreign-language area where an open attitude is prerequisite to learning.

By way of conclusion, we might offer a word of consolation in advance, for despite all the careful planning, there will certainly be some unforeseen problems which must be solved on the spot. FLES is not different in this respect from the rest of the school curriculum. If careful planning cannot do away with problems, however, it can do much to facilitate their handling by providing clear lines of communication and general policy as a basis for particular decisions. The most skilled classroom teacher is helpless without a general unified philosophy and efficient administration, but that same teacher must also actively acquire a sympathetic understanding of administrative problems, evidence a willing cooperation in their solution, and increase his own professional growth.

Chapter X

Two Programs

The ideas and examples presented in the previous chapters have been drawn from a variety of educational situations. Each FLES teacher, however, teaches in a real and individual situation: his aims and techniques must be made compatible to a general philosophy; the organization of his course is dependent upon the particular arrangements in his system. Therefore, we shall include brief descriptions of two specific situations, not because they are necessarily ideal, but simply because they are dynamic programs characterizing the kind of adjustments that must be made.

These two programs differ from each other as their communities differ. They were inspired at different times and grew from different educational thinking. Their growth and success have been characterized and influenced in great measure by the communities they serve and the kind of participation they sought and received from the community. With all these differences, however, they both work toward a common educational goal: high quality teaching of a foreign language and its culture in the elementary schools.

THE CLEVELAND PROGRAM

In 1922, when Cleveland instituted its Major Work Program for gifted children in the elementary grades, the possibility of an entirely new subject-matter and a new approach to the normal curriculum were considered.[1] The decision was reached to give these children training in foreign language in addition to their regular classes. The reasoning was that gifted children could do what is required of them more quickly than normal children and could be stimulated and rewarded by the study of a material well within their mental grasp and yet rarely taught to their age group. There was no implication in this "experiment" that foreign-language study requires exceptional capacity in children under twelve years old. Rather, the thought was that foreign-language learning is well adapted to that age group and such objections as "stealing time" for it were not at all valid for the exceptional child. The Cleveland FLES Program has, therefore, for over forty years been closely associated with the Major Work Program for the gifted child. In addition, a second phase, called Enrichment classes, has evolved from the Major Work Program.

When the children are tested, usually during the second grade, those testing 125 I.Q. or above are admitted to the Major Work Program and are permitted to go to the nearest school acting as a Major Work Center. Enrichment classes may be formed when a sufficiently large number of children testing 110-125 I.Q. are found attending a given school. These classes participate in the FLES program and are taught by the same specialist French teachers who teach the Major Work group; they follow the same course of study. The teacher's experience and judgment are vital factors with the Enrichment groups, for he must decide the exact portion of the Major Work Program which can be accomplished by each group at the standard high level of language excellence.

The methods and many of the techniques of teaching FLES in Cleveland were worked out experimentally long before World War II, when foreign-language teachers in America generally knew less about

---

[1] For a complete discussion of the Major Work Program, see Theodore Hall, *The Cleveland Story* (Cleveland: The World Publishing Co., 1956).

the science of linguistics than they do today. The Cleveland Plan, which is the general method used in all levels of Cleveland's language program, has been used in the FLES program. A single philosophy and method for all foreign-language teaching from grades three through twelve is thus assured. Such unity also eliminated completely one major pitfall in articulation to secondary work, that of the student's confusion at completely different demands made upon his knowledge and skills in the foreign language.

The Cleveland Plan is based on an active manipulation of four skills involved in language learning: hearing, speaking, reading, and writing, in that order. At the elementary school level, teaching is confined to the first two of these skills. Inductive reasoning plays an important role in language learning at all levels. The child is led to the proper conclusion, but he is given the privilege of drawing the conclusion and the satisfaction resultant to his success. Pattern drills, repetition with variety, total use of the foreign language in the classroom, all have been outstanding characteristics of the teaching since the beginning. The elementary program in French is based upon the philosophy that a child can acquire an acceptable pronunciation and some degree of fluency in a foreign language before the age of twelve providing he is taught by the audio-lingual method. Structure is introduced when he is sufficiently mature intellectually to profit by a more formal study of the language.

The Cleveland Plan employs a multiple approach to learning: the ear, the tongue, the eye, the hand, to which Dr. de Sauzé[2] added the principles of interest, selection of material, association, single emphasis, the inductive process, challenge, repetition, spontaneity, and incubation.

The material to be taught is carefully selected. The child's experience in the new language is focussed upon his daily activities; he is taught how to express in the foreign language his daily life at school and at home. "When a student learns a new language, instead of introducing him to a new experience, to a new story, foreign customs, for instance, it is much simpler to lead him to transfer his acquired experience from his mother tongue to the new language. He is learn-

---

[2] Cleveland appointed a Director of Foreign Languages in 1918, becoming one of the first large cities in the country to take such a step. It was Dr. Emile B. de Sauzé who received this appointment and served continuously until his retirement in 1949.

ing a second mode of expressing this same experience."[3] This principle is quite naturally expanded through contrast between the child's own experience and that of his French counterpart. The vocabulary is carefully chosen. Concrete words are associated with actions, pictures, objects or other words in a sentence. The sentence is the unit of thought and not the word. One new structural pattern is presented at a time. A reasonable amount of time is allowed for the pupil to assimilate what he has learned before going on to the next difficulty. The pupils are expected to pass from a stage of understanding to the stage of mastery before they go on to the next unit. New words and patterns are introduced by paraphrasing as opposed to an explanation in English. The new pattern can frequently be illustrated or given a visual image. Dr. de Sauzé considered the explanation in the foreign language far superior to the visual image because it presents the element of challenge: it stimulates the thinking of the pupil. It also helps the student to associate the new pattern with other related patterns. The child repeats a new expression until it becomes automatic and then spontaneous. This point cannot be emphasized too strongly.

The Cleveland course of study has been organized around the idea that the foreign language is to be the only medium of instruction. Teachers have found that time is actually saved rather than wasted by using the foreign language exclusively; that an atmosphere conducive to learning the language is thereby created; that it stimulates both the teacher and the pupils to express themselves in the language; and that if the use of English is permitted at all, the tendency is to use it too frequently. The course of study is the skeletal framework for the teacher's planning since it supplies the subjects for study and the structural patterns to be used. At the same time it allows the teacher to display creative ability in originality of presentation and development of the material.

Like every other school system which has instituted a FLES Program, Cleveland has had certain administrative problems to resolve over the course of years. As the program continues to grow and evolve, new adjustments are being made constantly. For example, a FLES Program in German was introduced during the academic year 1962-1963. Possibilities are currently being explored for a similar program

---

[3] Emile B. de Sauzé, *The Cleveland Plan for the Teaching of Foreign Languages* (New York: Holt, Rinehart & Winston Co., 1953), p 5.

in Spanish in an area of the city where such a program might have a real cultural and academic impact.

Briefly, the administration of the program is as follows. All teachers are certified foreign-language teachers. In the early days, these teachers were trained in foreign-language methodology for secondary teaching, but they were particularly interested in work with younger children. In 1960 Ohio was one of the first states to certify foreign-language teachers for grades one through twelve by means of a secondary certificate and two education courses pertaining to the elementary level, or elementary certification plus a major in the foreign language. Many of the Cleveland FLES teachers today are so certified and occasionally they move from level to level. Such adaptability is considered healthy for the system in that it breaks down any sense of isolation on individual levels.

All Cleveland FLES teachers are traveling specialists. Normally a teacher goes to two elementary schools in a day: one in the morning and another in the afternoon. The program may vary slightly with the size of the building or the number of classes, but normally a teacher will teach ten one-half hour periods per day. All classes, both Enrichment and Major Work, are one-half hour in length and meet five days a week. The Major Work groups average fifteen to a French class, for the group of thirty is divided for French. Normally too, the French teacher has his own classroom in each building. The children seem to like the idea of a place where they speak only French. The teacher is also free to decorate the room appropriately and has a place to store his visual aids.

The division into morning and afternoon schools minimizes the travel-time problem in the heavy city traffic. Naturally, effort is made to place a teacher in two schools in the same area of the city. At present there are eighteen full-time teaching positions in FLES in Cleveland and these are filled by twenty individuals. Cleveland has found that some certified teachers who for various reasons prefer only half-time teaching can be used with great efficiency and minimal administrative adjustments in the elementary program. The FLES teachers, as well as all the secondary teachers of foreign language are under the guidance and leadership of the Supervisor of Foreign Languages, Mr. Eugene K. Dawson.

At the junior high school level, only the Major Work and Enrichment classes have French in the first half-year. Classes for those who have had no previous foreign-language training are begun in the second half of the seventh grade, and are kept completely separate from the other group. A gifted child may add a second foreign language at that time or he may, after consultation with the counselor, change his foreign language or even drop it entirely for valid reason. In the senior high school, the students are grouped by performance in the language regardless of when they began, with advanced classes proceeding through the twelfth grade. One plaguing problem related to articulation remains constant, however: that of the transient American population. The constant testing program in the schools continually discovers children who have recently moved to Cleveland and who can profit from the FLES experience. These children enter the program in the elementary school years. In such cases, the experienced teacher needs to be vigilant to provide some success in order to avoid frustration and the resultant negative attitudes. For this reason, children found during the sixth grade are asked to wait to begin until junior high school on the basis that no language experience is better than a probable negative one.

Over the years Cleveland has had wide community interest in its FLES Program. In the early years, the Women's City Club was very helpful in promoting interest. By now many of the parents eager for their children to have this experience as part of their early education are persons who hold this conviction from personal experience. A number of French teachers in the Cleveland area are likewise people who began French "at the optimum age."

THE YORK PROGRAM

The York Program began in the early years of the FLES movement as a limited experiment which gradually developed into a citywide undertaking with certain unique characteristics. The idea of a foreign language program in the Pennsylvania city originated in connection with a workshop for parents and teachers organized under the aegis of the York public schools. A visiting speaker addressing this group in January, 1952, inspired those present with the ambition to inaugurate the teaching of a foreign language in the city's elementary schools. As a result Dr. Theodore Andersson, then director of the "Master of Arts in Teaching" program at Yale University, was invited in May of the same year to act as consultant during the initial planning of York's FLES venture. A decision was reached at that time to organize an experiment in the teaching of French to two second grade classes in one of the elementary schools of the city. The purpose of the undertaking was exploratory, but the hope was that the plan might be extended to include all the elementary school children in the York system.

A professional elementary school teacher on the instructional staff of the York school system was invited to take charge of the experiment and thus York's FLES classes from the very start functioned within the framework of a regular elementary school curriculum, making it possible to provide for continuity of program throughout the elementary grades.

The experimental classes were successful, and as a result, public interest in the teaching of a foreign language was heightened. A request was made for the organization of an adult French class; since that time a French class for adults has been offered each year in York.

Twenty new classrooms had been designated for FLES instruction during the school year 1953–1954; in 1955 still more classes were added in the West End area of the city. The adult classes were also continued. The following year the elementary program was extended to still more schools, this time in the eastern section of the city.

In May 1957, an evaluation committee headed by the assistant superintendent of schools submitted a favorable report of the FLES program to the Board of Education which then voted to extend the teaching of French to all the children of the city. In carrying through this decision budgetary considerations necessitated certain administrative choices, and the board members decided that *continuity of experience,* once a pupil had entered upon the program, was more important than an early start in studying the language. It was therefore decided to offer French beginning in the fifth grade rather than in the earlier grades and to extend the program through the junior high school to articulate with the existing language program in the high school.

A significant change in policy has developed in the last few years as a result both of experience and expediency. In the earlier years of the program the foreign language was offered to every York pupil, regardless of his academic competence. It has become evident to observers that elementary school classes made up of less talented students did not profit a great deal from their experience with FLES, while at the same time the junior high school program was not adequately staffed. Therefore at the present time, French is taught to the upper homogeneous classes in the larger elementary units and to all the heterogeneously grouped fourth, fifth, and sixth grades. The teaching is shared by a corps of six traveling language specialists who visit every class three times a week operating on a carefully planned schedule. This work is supplemented and reinforced by a weekly television program conducted by a member of the staff and carefully coordinated with the classroom teaching.

A unique feature of the York program is that it operates under a "twinning" plan in cooperation with the city of Arles, France, a community of comparable size and local interests. All the city schools of York including the Catholic high school, the junior college, the York County Day School, and some of the Girl Scout units of the city and county have participated in the twinning arrangement. In Arles "le Collège Technique, le Collège de Jeunes Filles, le Collège Frédéric Mistral, le Pensionnat St. Charles" and all the elementary schools take part. English is taught daily in the schools of Arles by six traveling specialists.

The children of the two cities correspond as "pen pals", exchange gifts and exhibits, and take a lively interest each in the other's activities. For several years there has been an exchange of teachers between the school system of Arles and that of York, Pennsylvania.

As a matter of fact the "twinning" arrangement between the two cities is not limited to their respective schools. It is actually a twinning of two city cultures. It involves not only exchange of correspondence, gifts, and teaching personnel, but also periodic exchange of personal visits by numerous citizens of each locality. Thus the abundance of "realia" of every sort; the frequent presence of real people from Arles, France, or York, U.S.A.; and the chance that the school children in the twinned communities enjoy to make friends with their peers across the ocean through continued correspondence have greatly enriched the teaching of culture in the paired cities. A reviewer of the first course of study in *Cités Unies*, the publication of the United Towns Organization, has expressed it thus:

> York a pu donner aux expériences FLES de ses écoles la motivation si souvent réclamée. Grâce au jumelage, l'enseignement du français à York connut, non seulement la motivation sentimentale créée par les perspectives de voyages ou de visites, ou par correspondance scolaire, génératrice d'amitiés pour la vie—mais aussi la présence toute concrète de Français d'origine.[5]

[5] "Un Manuel pas comme les autres," *Cités unies*, No. 11 (May 1959), 29.

Games, Activities & Songs

Many a good class has been taught without any game, song, or dance. The subject matter and the varied learning activities have been so interesting that the omission was never noticed. When this is the case we may assume that the teacher has real empathy with young children and is thus able to gear all of his classwork to their abilities and interests. However, all children love to play games, given a chance, and games serve as a delightful way of providing practice in using a foreign language. They are fun also for the teacher, provided he does not make the mistake of losing control of the class nor permit the youngsters to expect that they will be entertained all the time. He should never become so impressed by the importance of teaching a foreign language that he forgets how important play is in the life of the elementary school pupil or how valuable pleasant experiences are to the learning process itself. He should always remember that there is good evidence to show that young learners progress better when motivated by the prospect of a pleasant reward for success than when they work under the threat of unpleasant consequences as the result of failure. A game may be an appropriate reward while being a camouflaged review. By definition, any game used in a FLES class will have a linguistic rationale. Simply translating the unessential utterances of a familiar game cannot be defined as educational activity useful in a language period. The focal point of the worthwhile game will remain verbal communication by means of common linguistic structural patterns well within the range of a child's normal verbal expression. Once the teacher has verified these requirements to his own satisfaction, he may consider its other qualities of reward, activity, fun for the children.

SUGGESTIONS FOR THE FLES TEACHER

Here are some suggestions for the FLES teacher, whose class time with each group is limited and who works with pupils for whom other teachers have the major responsibility.

1. All games should involve the active linguistic participation or at least the attention of the whole class.

2. The teacher must be careful to explain a new game clearly and carefully so that, once started, it will move fast. A game must be fun and may be ridiculous from the standpoint of an uninitiated adult, but it must never be boring.

3. Any game having several variations should be introduced in its simplest form first. Only after it has been played and enjoyed and the children have the security of knowing the basic rules well, should variations be suggested.

4. In addition to providing the class with a change of pace and an enjoyable "fun time," games give the incentive and opportunity to practice structural patterns through automatic use.

5. Usually, the teacher should introduce the game and lead it until the pupils have become familiar with the procedure. Then he should hand the responsibility over to the class by asking *Qui veut prendre ma place?* Generally the first volunteer should be permitted to lead.

6. Games frequently encourage shy children to come forward. Pupils who hesitate to assume a role in a planned scene or fail to join easily in conversations with the teacher or other members of the class may actually volunteer to lead a game and do so successfully. The responsibility of giving directions so that the group may have fun helps these youngsters forget themselves and lose their inhibitions. Experienced teachers know how to appreciate and use such instances in helping diffident children develop leadership qualities.

GAMES FOR THE FIRST YEAR

MONTRE UN CROCODILE ORANGE

Although not actually a game, this activity provides an opportunity for action and for drill on colors. Using white construction paper, the teacher has cut out the outline of various animals, the names of which have been learned, such as *le chien, le chat, l'éléphant, le lapin, le poisson.* These outlines may be placed against colored paper to produce animals of different colors. The teacher will place the cut-outs and the colored paper on a table in the front of the room and say, *Montre un crocodile orange, Richard.*

VARIATION

The entire class may issue the commands according to the prompting of the teacher.

CLASS: Jean, lève-toi. Vas à la table. Montre le poisson.

TEACHER: De quelle couleur est le poisson?

A PUPIL: Le poisson est vert. (Jean must select the green.)

TEACHER: Qu'est-ce que tu montres?

JEAN: Je montre un poisson vert.

TEACHER: Jean, appelle une petite fille. (Jean takes the teacher's place and continues.)

JEAN: Montre l'éléphant, Marie, etc.

When all the animals have been chosen, the teacher sends the children to the board, one at a time, in this way, *Monsieur le Tigre, au tableau!* When all the children holding animals are at the board, someone can name them as follows: "*le poisson vert, l'éléphant bleu, le chien brun, le chat violet, etc.*"

TEACHER: Le chat violet, c'est effrayant!

CLASS: Ah non, Monsieur. Ce n'est pas effrayant. C'est drôle!

Various pupils may be asked to give their animals to others.

CLASS: Jean, donne le poisson vert à Guillaume.

JEAN: Voilà un poisson vert pour toi.

GUILLAUME: Merci beaucoup.

JEAN: De rien.

JE TAPE AVEC LE STYLO

The teacher taps on the board with a pencil, a pen, or a piece of chalk saying, *Je tape (frappe) avec le stylo sur le tableau. Combien?* The children count silently and raise their hands. The class is divided into two teams and the score is kept. The teacher may write G for the boys and F for the girls saying at the same time *J'écris G pour les garçons et j'écris F pour les filles.* The teacher is expected to call upon one team and then the opposing one until the correct answer is given. At the end of the game he will ask *Combien de points pour les jeunes filles? pour les garçons?* and will not write the number until a pupil has told the score. Then he will announce *Les garçons ont gagné. Très bien pour les garçons!* This game can be played very early in the first year and will surely be a success.

JE VOIS QUELQUE CHOSE

Definite preparation is necessary for this game. When the children have learned colors and are learning the articles of clothing, the game will provide repetitive drill without boring them. The teacher will go around the class indicating the clothing of some of the pupils and saying, *la robe de Marie, la jupe de Sylvie, le pantalon de Robert,* etc. The pupils repeat after the teacher or say it with him. Individual pupils are given a chance to practice in answer to the question *Qui veut répéter?*

Now the teacher begins the game by saying *Je vois quelque chose de brun dans la classe. Qu-est-ce que c'est?* Pupils volunteer the answer with another question *Est-ce la porte? Est-ce la chemise de Max?* The pupil who guesses correctly will automatically take the teacher's place. He is told in English that his choice of words must be confined to their French vocabulary and must be visible in the classroom.

JEU DE DEVINETTE, OUI ET NON

The guessing game *Oui et Non* may be used to advantage in the early part of the first year as a means of helping the pupils remember three basic structural patterns and several nouns. This type of game shows how many words have been mastered well enough to be used readily without help from the teacher. For this reason the teacher may use it as a disguised test. A pupil leaves the room while the class chooses an object in the room which they have included in their growing French vocabulary. The leader returns to the room and asks, *Est-ce un livre?* The leader is allowed only three questions. If he fails to guess correctly, the class tells him the answer, *Non, ce n'est pas le bureau. C'est la porte.* All three forms must be used correctly. The children learn the negative form very quickly through playing this game.

JE PENSE A DEUX NOMBRES

This game can be introduced without any explanation. It should be preceded by drill on numbers to 20 and simple addition facts. The leader will say *Je pense à deux nombres qui font onze. Lesquels sont-ils??* writing 11 on the board with a line above it and two question marks to indicate an addition combination. A pupil will say *Est-ce six et cinq?* and the teacher will say *Non, ce n'est pas six et cinq,* writing the numbers in place of the question marks. As the pupils suggest various possible combinations, the teacher will write them on the board. The pupil who guesses the correct combination has the privilege of leading the game.

The whole class will want to repeat *Je pense à deux nombres qui font . . .* for practice. As the game continues, the correct combinations remain on the board while the others are erased. After several pupils have led this game, the combinations on the board may be read by the class. Individual pupils may be sent to the board with the command *Vas au tableau, Sylvie. Efface trois et quatre.* Sylvie says *Je vais au tableau. J'éfface trois et quatre.*

JE PENSE A UN JOUR

When days of the week have been introduced, this amazingly simple game is enjoyed by a first-year class. The teacher will say *Je pense à un jour. Qu'est-ce que c'est?* A pupil asks *Est-ce jeudi?* The one who guesses correctly becomes the leader. The game provides practice in learning the days at a time when it is most needed. Later the game may be further enhanced by saying something about the day as *Je pense à un jour. La famille va à l'église. Quel jour est-ce?* or *Les enfants jouent* or *C'est un jour de fête en hiver. Quel jour est-ce?*

J'AI CINQ COULEURS

The teacher holds five strips of colored paper behind him saying *J'ai cinq couleurs derrière le dos. Dites une couleur.* A pupil says *le noir.* Then without looking the teacher pulls out one of the colors and says, *Est-ce le noir?* If the teacher happens to have pulled out a yellow paper, the pupil answers, *Non, ce n'est pas le noir. C'est le jaune.*

The first pupil who guesses the color correctly takes the teacher's place.

LE PERE NOEL ET QUATRE ENFANTS

Four cutouts of wooden shoes are placed on a table. The name of a child is written on each wooden shoe. Each pupil stands beside his shoe and takes the slip of paper which is under it. On this paper a toy has been drawn.

PAUL:	J'ai un train.
ANDRÉ:	J'ai une voiture.
SUZETTE:	J'ai une poupée.
JEANINE:	J'ai une bicyclette.
PÈRE NOËL:	Prenez vos jouets.

CLASS:	Merci, Père Noël.
PAUL:	Je suis heureux.
ANDRÉ:	Moi aussi.
CLASS:	Nous avons de beaux jouets.
	Vive Noël! Joyeux Noël! Bonnes vacances!

UNE CARTE POUR PERE NOEL

Pictures of toys and gifts which represent learned vocabulary should be displayed. The teacher will distribute a half sheet of paper to each pupil. Each will quickly sketch two or three things he wants for Christmas. The children should be limited to their French vocabulary. Each pupil writes his name on the bottom of the paper. The teacher collects the papers and draws several from the group. The pupils whose papers have been selected should tell what they have drawn on their papers saying, *Pour Noël je voudrais un camion, un avion, et une voiture.* A pupil may take the teacher's place in leading this game. He may say *Qu'est-ce que tu voudrais pour Noël?*

DES ORDRES—A VERB DRILL

Sheets of colored paper, pictures of animals, clothing or food or small objects found in the classroom or Christmas presents which are included in the vocabulary to be taught are displayed in front of the room. This exercise is useful for teaching the verb forms, *Je prends, je mets, je cherche, je donne;* colors such as *vert, gris, rouge, rose;* and the position of adjectives. The teacher will say, *Paul, prends le gros chien noir. Mets le gros chien noir sur la chaise. Sylvie, prends le gros livre vert. Donne le gros livre vert à Michèle.* After all articles have been placed by the children, give additional commands. *Joseph, cherche le petit chien brun et blanc. Donne le petit chien à Alain.*

The teacher may place these articles throughout the room while the pupils hide their eyes. Then the teacher will say, *Ouvrez les yeux, tous. Cherchez le petit livre gris.* A pupil volunteers and the game is carried on as before. This game helps to prepare the children for "*Simon dit.*"

IMITE-MOI

This game can be taught without any explanation in English. It involves movement on the part of the pupils and a good memory. Each pupil who participates imitates his predecessor and adds an action. The teacher should start it by saying *Je me lève, je touche le bureau*, and then *imite-moi*, indicate a pupil. The game should move fast, and the list of actions should not be too long.

CE QUE JE FAIS

Another game with motions which must move fast is a kind of abbreviated daily program. The entire class enacts the activities of the day. The game begins with the children pretending to be asleep and may end with them going home for lunch. *Je dors. Je me lève. Je me brosse les dents. Je dis, "Bonjour, Maman!" Je vais à l'école* (marching around the room). *Je fais du calcul. Je dessine. Je dis "Au revoir" à Monsieur. Je rentre chez moi. Je déjeune chez moi.*

QU'EST-CE QUE JE FAIS?

A pupil stands before the class and pantomimes an action such as eating an apple. He asks, *Qu'est-ce que je fais?* A pupil answers, *Tu manges une pomme.* The child who has answered correctly becomes the next leader.

DES AVIONS

Drill in learning numbers may be provided in the use of folded paper airplanes. Large numbers may be written inside the folded section or on the side of the plane. Pupils hide their eyes while a member of the class places the airplanes on their desks. They then read the numbers and show them to the class.

PIGEON VOLE

Pigeon vole and *Simon dit* require the identification of names and commands. At first it may be necessary to make these statements rather slowly in order to give the class an opportunity to recall.

They will be able to react quickly when the material has been well learned. The next step, of course, is for a pupil to take the teacher's place.

Pigeon vole may be introduced as soon as the pupils have learned some names of animals and birds. No explanation is needed. One day after talking about animals the teacher simply starts the game by saying, *Levez-vous, tous! Nous allons jouer à pigeon vole.*

Showing a picture of a pigeon, he says, *Pigeon vole!* and flaps his arms in a flying motion. Children do the same. Sometimes they enjoy repeating the statement. Then he shows a picture of a horse and says, *Cheval vole!* flapping his arms. When the children start to imitate the motion, he says, *Ah non! Le cheval ne vole pas! Asseyez-vous Charles et Robert.* He continues this procedure with *Chien vole, Chat vole,* while the children refuse to fly. Those who make a mistake are *hors du jeu.* Then he may say, *Dinde vole. Oiseau vole,* with pictures and continues with familiar nouns such as *Bureau vole. Chaise vole,* etc. Once the children have caught on, this game must move fast. They love it. Several names of new animals may be added to the known vocabulary in this way.

Older pupils like to play this game as it is done in France. Pupils remain seated with one hand on the desk. The index finger is the pigeon. The pupil raises his index finger to indicate that the bird flies.

A variation of this game, *Poisson nage,* may be played with an older group after a unit on vacations or a study of the language chart *Au Bord de la Mer.* It affords an opportunity to review the noun vocabulary: *Poisson nage, jeune homme nage, jeune fille nage, frère nage, soeur nage, bébé nage, oiseau nage, papa nage, dinde nage, éléphant nage, chien nage, bureau nage, chat nage, crocodile nage, maison nage, poisson rouge nage.*

SIMON DIT

Pupils are quick to realize that *Simon dit* is the French version of Simon says. The class obeys the commands of the leader only if they have been preceded by *Simon dit.* Anyone who makes a mistake is out of the game, *Robert, assieds-toi. Tu es hors du jeu!* Quite often the pupils automatically say what they are doing when the mistake is made, but this is not required. Some commands which may be used are *Touchez les oreilles, levez-vous, levez une main, levez le pied, regardez à gauche, fermez les yeux, baissez le pied, levez la main droite, touchez les pieds, levez-vous, mettez les mains sur la tête, sautez.* Individual pupils enjoy leading this game. This game is frequently played in a circle.

This activity provides an opportunity for use of negative commands. For example, *Simon dit, ne touchez pas le dos, ne fermez pas les yeux, n'ouvrez pas le bureau.*

Two pupils may play this game, one acting as the leader and the other, the pupil who obeys. *Simon dit: montre la tête, ne touche pas le bureau, va au tableau, écris zéro sur le tableau, n'efface pas le zéro, retourne à ta place, assieds-toi vite.*

The procedure may be reversed and children may take turns giving commands to the teacher. The pupil says, *Écrivez onze, Monsieur, prenez un papier, mettez le papier sur la tête, merci beaucoup.* This is a popular game which provides excellent drill in verbs as the pupil leader must master the difference between the less familiar imperative forms and the first person singular, which has now become a habit for him. Instead of saying *Je touche le dos* he must say *Touchez le dos* when addressing the class or the teacher and *Touche le dos* when speaking to one pupil.

During the second year any action verbs which have been learned may be used, *Chantez, marchez, comptez, lancez une boule de neige, cherchez un crayon, jouez à la balle, patinez.*

All the common commands may be reviewed by playing this game in the sixth grade in preparation for the use of *vous* in junior high school.

HUMOROUS SCENE

One child is sent out of the room, knocks at the door and the following abbreviated scene is enacted with much feeling:

CLASS	CHILD
Qui est là?	C'est moi!
Qui ça, moi?	Moi, Robert.
Entre, Robert.	Bonjour, tout le monde!
Bonjour, ferme la porte!	Bon, je ferme la porte.
Vas au tableau.	Non, je ne veux pas!
Eh bien, quitte la classe!	Bon, je quitte la classe.
Au revoir, ferme la porte!	Au revoir tout le monde!

VERSES FOR JUMPING ROPE

A la salade je suis malade,
Au céleri je suis guéri—
Lundi, mardi, mercredi, jeudi, vendredi, samedi, dimanche.
Janvier, février, mars, avril, mai, juin, juillet, août, septembre,
octobre, novembre, décembre.

Une souris verte
Qui courait dans l'herbe,
Je l'attrape par la queue
Je la montre à ces messieurs.
Ces messieurs me disent
"Trempez-la dans l'huile,
Trempez-la dans l'eau,
Ça fera un escargot tout chaud."

La soupe aux choux se fait dans la marmite.
Dans la marmite se fait la soupe aux choux.
(As one child jumps out on the word *choux*, another jumps in.)

LA BOITE MAGIQUE

This is a large box containing small objects or pictures of the
vocabulary that has been taught during the current year. The *Boîte
Magique* is introduced at the end of the first unit. It is used every
week and is kept up to date throughout the year. As the old material
is reviewed and the new is introduced pictures or objects are put into
the box.

Procedure for the use of this box is quite simple. Volunteer pupils
come in front of the class, and draw from the box. They then tell
something about the objects or pictures they have drawn and show
them to the class. As alternate activity a pupil may take the box
around the class allowing those in their seats to draw from it.

At Christmas time the box takes the form of *Un Sabot de Noël*
containing only Christmas material and at Easter time it becomes *Un
Oeuf de Pâques*.

After writing has been introduced, simple sentences or phrases may
be printed under some pictures but this enjoyable activity should
never become a mere reading exercise. It serves as a continuous review
of previously learned material.

CACHE ET TROUVE

First-year pupils enjoy playing this game in its simplest form. A pencil, a piece of chalk, a box, a small car or truck or any object is just barely hidden while one pupil is out of the room. When the pupil returns, the class asks the question *Où est le crayon?* and the pupil looks for the object and describes its location. If he cannot supply the correct answer, he loses the privilege of choosing the next player to leave the room and the one to hide the object. It is advisable to hide a different object each day the game is played. A few suggested answers are: *La voiture est dans le bureau, sous le bureau, sur la table, dans la bibliothèque, dans la grosse boîte.* The dialogue is as follows:

TEACHER:	Voulez-vous jouer?
CLASS:	Oui, Monsieur.
TEACHER:	A quoi voulez-vous jouer?
CLASS:	A Cache et trouve.
TEACHER:	Qui veut sortir? (Jean is chosen and goes out of the room.)
JEAN:	Je sors de la classe. (Teacher hides the object.)
CLASS:	Entre, Jean.
JEAN:	J'entre dans la classe.
CLASS:	Où est la voiture? (Jean discovers it.)
JEAN:	La voiture est sur le téléphone.
TEACHER:	Choisis quelqu'un. (He does.) Choisis quelqu'un pour cacher la voiture. (He chooses another.)

It is fun to move a favorite animal or toy around the room. One pupil may place the dog and ask, *Où est le gros chien noir?* while another answers *Le gros chien noir est sur la table.* If his answer is correct, he may be the leader. This game is simple, yet instructive.

A VARIATION

All pupils hide their eyes. The leader hides an object such as a book. He stands before the class and says, *Levez la tête et ouvrez les yeux. Où est le livre?* Individual pupils ask, *Est-ce dans le bureau de Richard? Est-ce sur le plancher? Est-ce dans le sac de Mademoiselle?* The child who guesses correctly hides the object the next time.

The leader may hide the book and then remove it while the other pupils are hiding their eyes. Then the pupils guess where it had been placed. They will ask *Est-ce que c'était sous la table?* [1] This game provides an excellent review of prepositions and drill on a past tense. The correct use of pronoun subjects may also be taught with this game.

QUELQUES DEVINETTES

Riddles of this type require special preparation rather than explanation. They may be included in the study on animals and parts of the body. Pupils are asked to draw an animal as preparation for the next class. Individual pupils come before the class and describe their animals as follows:

Voici mon chien. C'est un gros chien. Il est noir et blanc. Il s'appelle Fido.

Voici un éléphant. Il est gros. Il est gris. Il a de grosses oreilles et quatre grosses pattes. Il a une grosse tête.

As usual the teacher will start the game. The following are some riddles for a first-year class:

Je pense à un petit animal. Il est brun et blanc. Il a de longues quatre grosses pattes et une petite queue. Qu'est-ce que c'est? (un éléphant)

Je pense à un petit animal. Il est brun et blanc. Il a de longues oreilles et une petite queue. (le chien)

Je pense à un gros animal. Il a une longue tête et une longue queue. Il a quatre petites pattes. Il est vert ou gris. (le crocodile)

C'est un gros animal sauvage. Il est noir. Les gardiens chassent cet animal. (le taureau)

Je pense à quelque chose pour les petites filles. Ça dort. Ça marche. (la poupée)

Je pense à quelque chose. Il est grand et vert. Il est dans le jardin. (un arbre)

C'est une pièce de la maison. Dans cette pièce il y a une cheminée et un canapé. (le salon)

C'est un oeuf vert. Il est bon. Les enfants mangent ces oeufs. Quelle sorte d'oeuf est-ce? C'est un oeuf de Pâques.

C'est un jour de fête. Le Père Noël arrive par la cheminée. Tout le monde dit "Joyeux Noël!" Quel jour est-ce? C'est Noël. C'est le jour de Noël.

C'est une couleur. C'est la couleur d'une robe dans la salle de classe.

---

[1] Elizabeth Keesee, *Modern Foreign Languages in the Elementary School* (Washington, D. C.: U. S. Government Printing Office, 1960), p. 52.

Riddles have proved a source of motivation and an effective means of testing comprehension. They stimulate everyone and the more capable pupils will be eager to challenge the class with riddles of their own. Other "*devinettes*" which have been recorded on tape may be presented to the class at the end of the year as part of the testing program. The pupils will welcome them.

GAMES FOR THE SECOND YEAR

JEU DE FACTEUR

In this game all the players are considered adults. The children have written their names and addresses in French on envelopes or sheets of paper. These have been collected and three of them have been given to the postman who comes in front of the class. The following dialogue ensues:

FACTEUR: Bonjour, tous.

CLASSE: Bonjour, Monsieur.

FACTEUR: J'ai des lettres pour vous. Comment vous appelez-vous, Monsieur? (to one pupil)

MICHEL: Je m'appelle Michel Smith.

FACTEUR: Où habitez-vous?

MICHEL: J'habite .... (name of city).

FACTEUR: Dans quelle rue?

MICHEL: Dans la rue ....

FACTEUR: Quel est le numéro de votre maison?

MICHEL: C'est quatre-vingt-dix.

FACTEUR: Voici une lettre pour vous, Monsieur.

MICHEL: Merci.

FACTEUR: De rien. (Je vous en prie.)

JEU DE KIM

This game may be used often as a control of familiar material. The teacher places four or five objects on the table. Kim (pronounced Keem) says, *Je mets un crayon, un livre, un drapeau, un papier et un stylo sur la table.* The children hide their eyes while the teacher quickly removes one of the objects. The pupils have to tell which object is missing. They must use the correct article and pronounce the word well. *Que manque-t-il? Il manque un drapeau.*

A variation of this game may be played with a large number of objects on the table. Kim will name them as he shows them to the class. Then a child is chosen to leave the room. Kim removes one of the objects. When the person who is "it" enters, the class asks him, *Que manque-t-il?* He will answer, *Il manque le petit chien.* To which the class will respond, *Oui, il manque le petit chien.*

Numbers may be substituted for objects. The leader counts always omitting one number. *Un, deux, trois, cinq. Que manque-t-il? Il manque quatre.*

FLUTE

The teacher will explain this game in French by saying *Aujourd'hui nous allons jouer à flûte avec sept. Dites "flûte"* (Everyone repeats it correctly several times being sure to pronounce the "u" well.) *Nous allons compter. Ne dites pas sept. Dites flûte.* While writing multiples of 7 on the board the class continues to count being sure to substitute *flûte* for 14. It is important for a class to see 21, 28, 35, etc., on the board when they are playing the game for the first time. Now the teacher starts with *Commence à compter, Jeanne.* Every child says only one number. Anyone who forgets to say *flûte* is *hors du jeu.* There should be time to go around the class at least twice. Most classes begin rather slowly but they are soon able to play the game at its proper speed.

DITES-MOI VITE!

This drill is a camouflaged review of numbers. Flash cards are used and speed is emphasized. The whole class stands. Each pupil takes his turn and may be seated as soon as he has named his number correctly.

ECRIS LE NOMBRE

The number game described here is suggested as a follow-up activity. The teacher will ask pupils who have missed a number to write that number on a quarter sheet of paper which has been provided by the teacher. *Comment dit-on* seventy-five, *Jacques?* . . . *Ecris un gros soixante-quinze sur le papier.* These papers are collected. The next day the papers are returned to the pupils. The teacher will say, *Soixante-quinze, lève la main. Cinquante-deux, sors de la classe. Seize, vas au tableau.* The pupils comply and tell what they are doing.

EFFACEZ!

Drill in the use of the negative and a review of numbers are provided by this short interesting game. The teacher has written duplicate columns of not more than ten numbers on the board. Volunteers representing each team go to the board. Now the teacher says, *Effacez quarante.* The pupil who erases the correct number first wins a point for his team. Other commands such as this follow: *N'effacez pas Vingt-et-un. Effacez Vingt-neuf. N'effacez pas trois. Effacez treize.*

UN MATCH

To help pupils remember the gender of nouns the procedure of *Dites-moi vite* is suggested for these two contests. A representative from each team will stand focussing his attention upon the teacher who will flash a picture or an object or he may say *jupe, un ou une?* The pupil who calls out the answer with the correct article first, wins a point for his team.

REGLEZ L'HORLOGE VITE!

Two pupils from opposing teams can write a dictated number on the board. The first one to write it correctly earns a point for his team. Two pupils may compete in the same way in setting the hands of two clocks as the teacher dictates the time to be shown. The class says *Réglez l'horloge vite!* Someone calls out a time and both pupils set their clocks as quickly as possible. This contest facilitates learning to tell time in French.

J'AI GAGNE!

Bingo! An ordinary Bingo set can be changed to include many of the higher numbers. This adaptation is an improvement over the commercial product. The French pronunciation of the letters "B,"

"I," "N," "G," and "O" is used. Either the teacher or a pupil can lead this game. At first another pupil may write all the numbers on the board as they are called. When a pupil has Bingo, he calls *J'ai gagné!* As he names the numbers they are checked by the caller. Small squares of colored paper or buttons may be used as *boutons*. This valuable and enjoyable game should be played two days in succession and should follow intensive number drill.

AS-TU LA BOITE?

The pupil who is "It" hides his eyes while a flat box is hidden in someone's desk. The pupil who is "It" asks, *Etes-vous prêts?* and the class answers, *Oui, nous sommes prêts.* "It" is allowed only three questions to find the box. He asks, *As-tu la boîte, Jean?* Jean must say, *Non, je n'ai pas la boîte.* If the three questions are unsuccessful, he asks the class, *Qui a la boîte?* The pupil who had it responds with *Moi, j'ai la boîte,* and becomes the next "It." Any small object may be hidden.

EFFACEZ QUELQUE CHOSE

Practice in saying *Il n'a pas de* is provided as preparation for this game. The teacher will draw an animal on the board, and will erase the feet and will help the class to say *Il n'a pas de pattes.* He will continue to erase one part of the body at a time until the pupils have learned the expression. Then he will draw another animal or a boy on the board and say to the class, *Fermez les yeux* and erase the nose. *Regardez le garçon. Qu'est-ce qu'il n'a pas?* The class will answer *Il n'a pas de nez.*

A pupil takes the teacher's place, tells the children to close their eyes, erases the ears, and tells them to open their eyes. Another pupil says *Il n'a pas d'oreilles.* It is best for the class to master this game completely before using the feminine pronoun.

NOUS ALLONS JOUER AU DETECTIVE!

To be thoroughly enjoyed this game must be presented step by step. It is appreciated most by second year pupils who have already learned to describe their clothing. The leader goes out of the room and the class chooses someone.

Step One

TEACHER: Jean, sors de la classe et ferme la porte.
(to class) Choisissez quelqu'un.

PUPIL: Je choisis Charles.

TEACHER: Comment est-il habillé?

PUPIL: Il a une chemise verte, un pantalon brun et des chaussures noires. (The description may be shared by three children, if necessary.)

CLASS: Entre, Jean.

JEAN: J'entre dans la classe. (not required)

PUPIL: Il a une chemise verte, un pantalon brun et des chaussures noires.

JEAN: Est-ce Charles? (He has three guesses. If he guesses correctly, he may choose the next leader.)

Step Two

Parts of the body have been learned and pupils are accustomed to saying *J'ai les cheveux courts. Je n'ai pas les cheveux longs.* The teacher prepares the class for step two by describing the hair of a few pupils who have been asked to stand in front of the class. The following sentences must be learned: *Il a les cheveux châtains, blonds, noirs. Elle a les cheveux longs, courts.*

This time the description will begin with the hair which is described by two pupils and the clothing is described as before.

Step Three

The teacher introduces *les yeux marrons, bleus, gris* by describing the eyes of various pupils. He may go around the room while the class describes the hair and eyes of some of the pupils. This practice is needed. Now the description includes hair, eyes, and clothing. Individual children each are made responsible for one sentence. They are standing when the leader returns to the room and they say their sentences one after another without looking at the chosen pupil. The leader listens, looks around the room and usually guesses the identity of the child very easily.

Step Four

The leader asks these questions:

Est-ce un garçon ou une jeune fille?

A-t-elle les cheveux longs?
A-t-elle les cheveux blonds?
A-t-elle une robe blanche et bleue? De quelle couleur est sa robe?
Est-ce Jeanne?

QUI SUIS-JE?

The pupil who is "It" hides his eyes or turns his back to the class.
Another taps him on the back and the following conversation
ensues:

Qui est là?
C'est moi.
Qu'est-ce que tu veux?
Je veux un livre. (Je voudrais)
De quelle couleur?
Je voudrais un livre bleu. Qui suis-je? (Devine!)
C'est toi, Paul?
Non, ce n'est pas Paul.

The pupil who is "It" may vary his question by saying, *Un gros
livre ou un petit livre? Un livre français ou anglais?* or *Veux-tu un
beau livre?* The first pupil may ask for anything, for example, *je
voudrais un jouet.—Quel jouet est-ce que tu veux?—Un petit camion
rouge.*

The pupil has three chances to guess the identity of the other
pupil. If he guesses correctly, the pupil who spoke takes his place
and the game continues. If he cannot guess correctly, another pupil
takes his place.

A variation of this game involves the imperfect tense. The pupil
who speaks returns quickly to his seat and the leader turns around
and asks *C'était toi, Edouard?* Edward answers *C'était* or *Ce n'était
pas moi.*

JEU DE DEVINETTE

Nous avons joué au détective avec des personnes. Maintenant nous
allons jouer au détective avec des objets. Le principe de ce jeu est de
situer l'objet. Je divise la classe en quatre parties, la droite et la
gauche, la devant et la derrière, en dessinant un carré qui représente
la classe.

Adequate preparation must be made before this guessing game

can be used. Only five questions should be asked by the leader. They are as follows:

De quelle couleur est-ce?
Est-ce gros ou petit?
Est-ce à droite ou à gauche?
Est-ce devant ou derrière la classe?
Est-ce le piano?

PUIS-JE?

One pupil commands another, but the second one may not fulfill the command until he has received permission a second time. This game provides excellent practice for future seventh graders who will have to ask permission to move around the room.

Ouvre le bureau, Jacques.
Puis-je?
Oui, tu peux. Ouvre le bureau.
Ecris ton nom.
Puis-je?
Non, tu ne peux pas. Assieds-toi.

RHYTHM, OR ZERO APPELLE SIX!

This game can be played best by approximately fifteen elementary pupils at a time. Each child is given a number. Children all keep the same rhythm by clapping both hands on their knees, then clapping their hands together, snapping the fingers of the left hand while one child says his own number and then snapping the fingers of the right hand. On this snap the same child says another student's number. The group continues slapping knees and clapping hands. On the left snap of the fingers the second child says his number, and on the right snap he says another child's number. The game continues in this manner and each time a different child has a turn. Anyone who misses a beat or calls the pupil who immediately preceded him is out.

UN MATCH

A contest or *match* between two teams provides motivation for drill which might otherwise become boring and stimulates competition in a review lesson. If the contest includes the recognition of

nouns, these five structural patterns should be used: Où est . . .?
Qu'est-ce que c'est? Est-ce un . . .? Touche. . . . Montre. . . . Three
nouns must be identified to gain one point.

As children continue in their second year of French, pupil leaders
are capable of asking many of the questions. Every class may be
divided into two teams. When a unit has been learned, a match is
conducted but the questions are no longer asked by the teacher alone.
Pupil leaders may ask some of the questions.

Older pupils prefer a more definite organization. The teacher may
wish to divide the class arbitrarily into two teams or the pupils may
be willing to have the boys compete against the girls. Each team will
select a captain and a name such as les tigres or les lions. The election
of the captains may easily be conducted in French. The rules of the
contest must be clear. If a captain calls upon a volunteer from his
own team who cannot supply the correct answer, he must call upon
a volunteer from the opposing team. The leaders take turns asking
the questions. Very keen competition usually results from this activity.
Cumulative scores are kept.

LE CLUB QUELLE HEURE EST-IL?

The team captains may be asked to cooperate in several lessons on
telling time. After some drill has been provided, the teacher will ask
the team captains to prepare a list of ten time questions for the next
day. The pupils who are able to answer two questions will become
members of the "Club quelle heure est-il?" and will win a point for
their team. Two frames are drawn on the board and the first captain
writes in the hours to be read in this way.

9:15   10:50
neuf heures et quart   onze heures moins dix

He calls upon a volunteer from his team first. Each team will try to
gain as many points as possible. The cumulative score is kept.

JOURS ET MOIS

The following are a few riddles suggested for more advanced elementary pupils. Pupils often display a great deal of originality in this
enjoyable activity. The first and last sentences remain the same in
each question.

1. Je pense à un jour. Les enfants français ne vont pas a l'école ce jour-là. Quel jour est-ce?

2. Ce jour-là je regarde la télévision à dix heures du matin.

3. Marie déjeune à la maison ce jour-là.

4. Robert va aux Eclaireurs. Il va nager ce jour-là.

5. C'est le premier jour de la semaine.

6. Je pense à un mois. Il fait froid. C'est l'hiver. Jean fait du ski. Quel mois est-ce?

7. Je patine. Il fait froid.

8. Les garçons jouent au football. Il fait frais.

9. Il fait beau. C'est le printemps. Les garçons jouent au baseball.

10. Il fait mauvais temps mais les garçons jouent au basket.

11. Je vais en vacances.

12. Je nage dans la mer. Il fait beau, et il fait chaud. Il fait du soleil. Tout le monde s'amuse.

13. Je retourne à l'école. C'est la rentrée des classes. Quel mois est-ce?

JOUR, JOUET, MOIS

A simple game of categories offers a challenging mental activity which appeals to the more talented pupils. It tests comprehension and provides practice in the negative form. Pupils must know the terms *jour, mois,* and *jouet* which are generally used in December and January when toys are discussed and the months of the year are taught.

The teacher will instruct the pupils as follows: *Levez la main quand je dis quelque chose qui n'est pas correct. Lundi est un jour, samedi est un jour, un train électrique est un jour. . . .* He will pause as the hands are raised and help the first pupil to say, *Non, un train électrique n'est pas un jour. C'est un jouet.* He will then continue with *Une poupée est un jouet. Un avion est un jouet. Une balle est un jouet. Novembre est un jouet.* When a pupil is able to form the correct statement himself, he will also be capable of leading the game.

Other worthwhile possibilities are *nombres, animaux, oiseaux, parties de la maison, couleurs, plantes.* This type of game should not consume too much time but it is instructive and enjoyable.

DRILL AND CONTEST

Step One

The teacher will prepare twelve flash cards each representing a month. He will flash them one at a time to the class for pupils to answer the question, *Quel mois est-ce?*

Step Two

Using the flash cards the teacher will ask, *Quel temps fait-il en décembre, en juillet?* etc.

Step Three

Using weather pictures pupils will ask each other the question, *Quel temps fait-il sur l'image?*

Il pleut.	Il fait mauvais.
Il fait du soleil.	Il fait froid.
Il neige.	Il fait chaud.
Il fait beau.	Il fait du vent.
Le ciel est bleu.	Le ciel est gris.
Il est couvert.	

Step Four

Devinez! The flash cards of the months are placed face downward on a table. A pupil selects one of these cards, looks at it and asks the class, *Il fait froid. Quel mois est-ce?* The one who guesses correctly becomes the next leader. Team captains may ask the questions and the procedure for a contest or match may be followed.

QUESTION AND ANSWER FLASHCARDS

Advanced elementary pupils enjoy an activity which involves sight reading of familiar material. Questions and answers are written on flashcards or typed on small sheets of paper.

The class is divided in half, the questions are distributed to one group and the corresponding answers to the other group. Individuals read their questions in French and the child holding the answer, reads it to the class. This activity gives sixth-grade students a fine feeling of achievement and strengthens their confidence. It has also proved effective and popular in junior high school.

BONNE ANNIVERSAIRE

Pupils' birthdays may be celebrated in a very simple manner approximating a real life situation. A large colorful drawing of a birthday cake may be presented to a pupil on his birthday. Before the event the following conversation ensues:

TEACHER: Quel âge as-tu, Jacques?

PUPIL: J'ai dix ans.

TEACHER: Quelle est la date de ton anniversaire?

PUPIL: Mon anniversaire est le vingt-et-un novembre.

TEACHER: Combien de bougies y aura-t-il sur ton gâteau?

PUPIL: Il y aura onze bougies sur mon gâteau.

The pupil in charge of birthdays for the month will present the cake to Jacques on his birthday saying:

PUPIL: Bonne anniversaire, Jacques.
Voici un gâteau pour toi.

JACQUES: Merci beaucoup.

The class sings "Bonne Anniversaire" to the familiar tune of "Happy Birthday to You!"

A RHYME

For the purpose of adding variety to classroom procedure the class may recite a rhyme as a means of choosing the leader of a game. Ten pupils are asked to stand in front of the class. A leader taps them as the rhyme is repeated, one syllable for each person. One pupil is eliminated at the end of every line and the remaining pupil will be "it." A popular verse for this kind of activity with young children is the French version of "Hickory, dickory, dock":

> I-go-ré, di-go-ré, doge.
> Le rat monte à l'horloge
> Une heure frappe!
> Le rat s'échappe!
> I-go-ré, di-go-ré, doge.[2]

---

[2] Elizabeth Gessler, *En Avant* (New York: Gessler Publishing Co., 1958). Reprinted by permission.

Included in this category are all kinds of jingles, verses, and devinettes.

Quite often a special password or structural pattern may be required of the children as they enter or leave the room.

SONGS

The games described above provide educational activity and indirect foreign-language instruction in a variety of ways. They also frequently strengthen the children's accuracy and rapidity in arithmetical functions. Songs and dances provide another type of correlating activity that is very much enjoyed by youngsters and is at the same time instructional in foreign language—music and coordinated physical movement. A further advantage is that many of the songs and dances provide group participation for relatively large numbers of children. The folklore repertory in this area is almost inexhaustible. The few examples we have chosen to present have proved their effectiveness and will serve to indicate the possibilities in this area for the enterprising teacher.

A few words of caution are perhaps in order. Some folklore music is unnecessarily complicated musically for children and may well require simplification for successful performance by the youngsters. Naturally, too, the vocabulary of the song needs to be controlled, for a lively, attractive air with totally unfamiliar lyrics will have little value in a FLES class. Finally, the action or dance step needs to be simple enough not to distract the child's attention from the other parts of the coordinated activity.

Normally children welcome this kind of activity—both because of its pleasing variety and because of its inherent charm as an expression of national culture.

LA GALETTE

J'ai-me la ga - let - te, Sa - vez vous com -ment?

Quand elle est bien fai - te A - vec du beurre de - dans.

Tra la la la la la la la lè - re, Tra la la la

la la la la lè - re, Tra la la la la la la la

lè - re, Tra la la la la la la la la.

From Edmée Arma, Et Maintenant Dansons ..., copyright 1949 by
Fernand Nathan Editeur, Paris. Reprinted by permission.

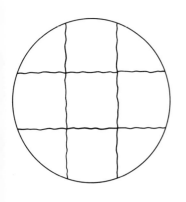

When taught in the recreation room, this
game is played as follows:

1. Pupils join hands and form a circle.
   One child in the center of the circle
   holds a large yellow paper "galette"
   high above his head. (See drawing.)
   On the first line children take little
   steps slowly toward the center of the
   circle, raising joined hands high over
   heads.
   On the second line they step backward.
   This activity is repeated for lines three
   and four.
   On "tra-la-la" all children clap hands
   or skip around in a circle.

2. Various activities may be introduced for each verse alternating between active and more quiet motions.
3. One time the boys may step forward, "Que les garçons!"

The next time the girls may come forward, "Que les jeunes filles!" When taught in the classroom, the following motions are suggested:

1. First line—Children clap hands against knees.
2. Second line—Children turn hands in air.
3. Repeat motions for lines three and four.
4. Skip around in a circle with partners for "tra-la-la."

YOUPI

You-pi You-pi est par-ti, Et m'a pris ma fi-an-cée. Mais je

me suis con-so-lé, En pre-nant celle d'à cô-té.____

____ Tra la la la la, Tra la la la

la, Tra la la la la, Tra la la la la.

Every pupil has a partner. Couples form a circle with boys on the outside. Youpi skips inside the circle, steals a girl and skips with her inside the circle. Everyone claps hands while Youpi and his partner dance or skip. Now they join the other players in the circle while the one who has no partner becomes the next Youpi.

French directions: *Mettez-vous en cercle. Placez-vous chaque garçon devant une petite fille (chaque garçon choisissez une fille.) Youpi, danse dans le cercle. Quand vous chanterez tra-la-la, Youpi choisira une petite fille et dansera avec elle pendant que les enfants frappent des mains.*

Also: *Mettez-vous en rond. Youpi, entre dans le rond.*

LE LAPIN

Dans sa mai - son   un grand cerf   Re - gar - dait   par

la   fe - nêtre   Un   la - pin   ve - nir   à   lui

Et   frap - per   ain - si: Cerf, cerf, ou - vre - moi

Ou   le   chas - seur   me   tu - era.   La - pin, la - pin,

rentr' et   viens   Me   ser - rer   la   main.

Pupils describe the following motions in the air:

Line 1—they describe a house and antlers
" 2—looking out the window
" 3—motions of a rabbit running and knocking on door
" 5—open the door
" 6—hunter ready to shoot
" 7—come in
" 8—shaking hands

MON MARRONIER

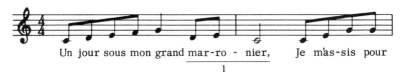

Un jour sous mon grand mar - ro - nier,   Je m'as - sis pour

1

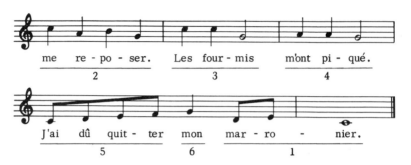

me re - po - ser. Les four - mis m'ont pi - qué.
2   3   4

J'ai dû quit - ter mon mar - ro - nier.
5   6   1

a. Teacher explains the song, and teaches it by rote.

b. Class stands and actions are introduced.
   First line: children place hands on shoulders and extend arms
                   upward to describe a tree.
   Second line: motion of sitting down.
   Third line: brushing clothes with hands, then brushing ants from
                   hands with a kind of clapping motion.
   Fourth line: motion of leaning and arms extended upward to
                   describe the tree.

c. The song is sung six times, each time omitting one more phrase until
   mon is sung alone in the last line. Then the seventh time pupils
   make all the motions without singing and the last time the entire
   song is sung.

RIRE
(Canon)

Ri–re, ri–re, ri–re, ri–re, Dans les bois et

dans les prés. Le beau temps re - vient. Il faut

ri - re ha, ha, ha, Ri - re dans les prés.

LA FILLE DU COUPEUR DE PAILLE
(Danse provençale)

Sur mon che-min j'ai ren-con-tré La fil - le du cou-

peur de pail - le. Sur mon che-min j'ai ren-con - tré

La fil - le du cou - peur de blé. Oui, oui, j'ai ren-con-tré

La fil - le du cou - peur de pail - le. Oui, oui,

j'ai ren-con - tré La fil - le du cou - peur de blé.

French directions for dancing:
Les garçons, faites une ligne droite.
Les jeunes filles, faites une ligne droite, aussi.
Chaque garçon, attrapez (tenez) les mains de chaque jeune fille.
Avancez; (measures 1, 2) reculez. (measures 3, 4) (This is repeated)
Lachez les mains et frappez les mains. (measure 9 to end)
Le premier couple passez entre les deux lignes (la rangée) en sautant
et retournez à la première place.

L'ALPHABET

A   B   C   D   E   F   G,   H   I

J   K   L   M   N   O   P,   Q   R   S   et

T   U   V,   Dou-ble V   X   I - grec   et

Z;   Là,   je   sais   mon   al - pha - bet;

Je   le   chan - te   en   fran - çais.

On prononce l'alphabet: a, bé, sé, dé, e (comme le), èf, jé (ghé), ache,
i (comme machine), ji, ka, èl, èm, èn, o, pé, ku, èrre, èss, té, u, vé,
double vé, iks, ī grec, zède.

From En Avant, copyright 1958 by the Gessler Publishing Co.,
110 E. 23rd St., New York 10, N.Y. Reprinted by permission.

LES VOYELLES

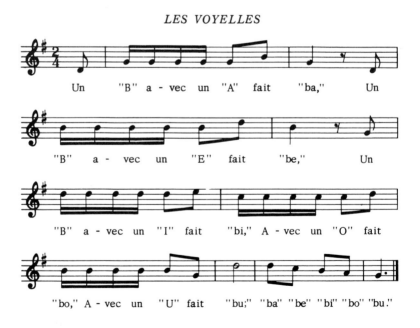

Un   "B" a - vec un "A" fait   "ba,"   Un

"B"   a - vec   un   "E" fait   "be,"   Un

"B"   a - vec un   "I" fait   "bi," A - vec un   "O" fait

"bo," A - vec un   "U" fait   "bu;" "ba" "be" "bi" "bo" "bu."

From En Avant, copyright 1958 by the Gessler Publishing Co.,
110 E. 23rd St., New York 10, N.Y. Reprinted by permission.

Appendix 2

Note on In-Service Training

No in-service program can accomplish miracles, but a well-planned program can go far in helping inadequately trained teachers to become more efficient in their work. Such a program may take the form of either a summer workshop or special sessions during the school year. Experience has shown that there are two specific areas in which further training may be helpful: 1. methods and techniques including audio-visual materials; 2. specific language competence. It is evident, of course, that NDEA summer institutes are doing very effective work in both of these areas, but they cannot satisfy the demand and, in some cases even now, individual FLES teachers cannot meet the minimal foreign language requirement for these institutes. On the other hand, the NDEA Institutes are providing widespread leadership through the key people they have trained. Within a particular community, it is common practice for teachers returning from NDEA Institutes to discuss their experience with the other FLES teachers of their community region. In addition, state supervisors of foreign languages have been able to provide leadership in meetings and workshops, especially on methodology and techniques of FLES teaching. This is especially true where a demonstration by a master teacher forms an integral part of the workshop.

Monthly staff meetings are a necessity in any program, but they can be particularly valuable where the efficiency of individual teachers is quite disparate. Cooperation is essential if any measure of coherence is to be achieved in such a program and such cooperation will depend in large measure on the tactful leadership of the coordinator. Specific help can be given on techniques for presenting material, in finding material, and in developing supplemental activities appropriate to the basic course materials. Some agreement must be reached on the amount of material that will be taught and the kind of testing program to be adapted. In the earlier stages of a program, teachers usually need help in the preparation and presentation of demonstration lessons. The preparation of good visual aids and the efficient use of audio aids are important aspects of FLES teaching that can be taken up at these meetings. Guidance is also needed on such vital questions as the minimal use of English, the timing of reading and writing, and the omission of analytic grammar.

Teachers may sometimes find it expedient to hold more frequent discussions of common problems, in some cases weekly meetings have done much to improve a FLES program. Although materials may be exchanged at these times, it is better that the preparation and distribution of materials not be the primary purpose of these meetings. The exchange of ideas and mutual help that members of the staff get from each other fortify each individual and strengthen the entire program. As new teachers are added to the group, they are oriented to the aims and philosophy of the FLES program as well as to the practical application of these ideas. Friendly observation of each other's classes may prove very helpful if it can be arranged.

Language competence, the second major area stressed by in-service programs has its own peculiar problems that also require delicate handling. In some instances, the inadequacy is closely tied to methodology, for example, ineffective teaching of pronunciation by a fluent or even native teacher. But more frequently, the fact is that the teacher himself is something less than an ideal linguistic model for his pupils' imitation. Or the problem may be that the teacher was not trained in an audio-lingual manner and does not feel at ease in leading the endless variety of pattern practice required to give the children a sense of easy fluency with precise pronunciation and intonation. In such situations a carefully planned language course should be organized for these teachers, using all the modern aids to language learning, such as tapes or records for home use and good programmed machine learning as it becomes available. The key to such a language course will obviously be the teacher. It is even possible that a system may choose to have two courses with two separate teachers. In such a case, one teacher completely familiar with the manual being taught in the FLES program would concentrate on pronunciation and drill of all varieties on the specific material being taught by the group in order to increase their efficiency both as model and as teacher. Such learning, while of immediate and telling importance in the classroom is, however, insufficient for an adult's complete grasp of the language. It is becoming common practice, therefore, in such in-service language courses to accompany this first level language course with a second audio-lingual course at an adult level. This second course will proceed beyond the level of the children to a satisfactory grasp of the complete structure of the language, some knowledge of the general culture of the country, and even an introduction to literature of the language. Such a series of courses permits the interested teacher to progress indefinitely and independently whether by courses at neighboring institutions of higher learning or by travel in the foreign country. Normally, at the end of a year, the teacher will no longer need the first course keyed to his specific material but may well profit from continued language work at an adult level. As the teacher gains ease, security, and fluency in the language he is teaching, he will become a more effective creative teacher.

There is one other important point about in-service programs. Occasionally such programs will uncover an enthusiastic teacher who, as an adult, has simply lost the power of aural perception and imitation necessary to language learning. Such persons should be dissuaded from continuing in FLES. They should, rather, be oriented to other forms of elementary teaching where their talents lie, for the teacher as model is basic to the FLES program.

MLA Competence Ratings
for Foreign-Language Teachers

The competences given below were defined by the Modern Language Association of America and should be applied to all modern foreign-language teachers.

COMPETENCE—AURAL UNDERSTANDING

Superior: Ability to follow closely and with ease all types of standard speech, such as rapid or group conversation, plays and movies.

Good: Ability to understand conversation of average tempo, lectures, and news broadcasts.

Minimal: Ability to get the sense of what an educated native says when he is enunciating carefully and speaking simply on a general subject.

COMPETENCE—SPEAKING

Superior: Ability to approximate native speech in vocabulary, intonation, and pronunciation (for example, the ability to be at ease in social situations).

Good: Ability to talk with a native without making glaring mistakes, and with a command of vocabulary and syntax sufficient to express one's thoughts in sustained conversation. This implies speech at normal speed with good pronunciation and intonation.

Minimal: Ability to talk on prepared topics (for example, for classroom situations) without obvious faltering and to use the common expressions needed for getting around in the foreign country, speaking with a pronunciation readily understandable to a native.

COMPETENCE—READING

Superior: Ability to read, almost as easily as in English, material of considerable difficulty, such as essays and literary criticism.

Good: Ability to read with immediate comprehension prose and verse of average difficulty and mature content.

Minimal: Ability to grasp directly (that is, without translating) the meaning of simple, nontechnical prose, except for an occasional word.

COMPETENCE—WRITING

Superior: Ability to write on a variety of subjects with idiomatic naturalness, ease of expression, and some feeling for the style of the language.

Good: Ability to write a simple "free composition" with clarity and correctness in vocabulary, idiom, and syntax.

Minimal: Ability to write correctly sentences or paragraphs such as would be developed orally for classroom situations, and to write a short, simple letter.

COMPETENCE—LANGUAGE ANALYSIS

Superior: Ability to apply knowledge of descriptive, comparative, and historical linguistics to the language-teaching situation.

Good: A basic knowledge of the historical development and present characteristics of the language, and awareness of the difference between the language as spoken and as written.

Minimal: A working command of the sound patterns and grammar patterns of the foreign language, and a knowledge of its main differences from English.

COMPETENCE—CULTURAL

Superior: An enlightened understanding of the foreign people and their culture, achieved through personal contact, preferably by travel and residence abroad, through study of systematic descriptions of the foreign culture, and through study of literature and the arts.

Good: First-hand knowledge of some literary masterpieces, an understanding of the principal ways in which the foreign culture resembles and differs from our own, and possession of an organized body of information on the foreign people and their civilization.

Minimal: An awareness of language as an essential element among the learned and shared experiences that combine to form a particular culture, and a rudimentary knowledge of the geography, history, literature, art, social customs, and contemporary civilization of the foreign people.

COMPETENCE—PROFESSIONAL

Superior: A mastery of recognized teaching methods, and the ability to experiment with and evaluate new methods and techniques.

Good: Ability to apply knowledge of methods and techniques to the teaching situation (for example, audio-visual techniques) and to relate one's teaching of the language to other areas of the curriculum.

Minimal: Some knowledge of effective methods and techniques of language teaching.

Foreign Languages in the Elementary School

A STATEMENT OF POLICY[1]

After more than three years of studying a variety of reports on the teaching of foreign languages in the public elementary schools, we express our approval of this popular movement in American education. In our judgment the movement deserves the support of parents and educational administrators because:

1. it recognizes the evidence concerning the process of language learning, introducing study of a second language to children at an age when they are naturally curious about language, when they have fewest inhibitions, and when they imitate most easily new sounds and sound patterns;

2. it recognizes the fact that real proficiency in the use of a foreign language requires progressive learning over an extended period.

---

[1] Reprinted from "FL Program Policy," *PMLA*, Vol. LXXI, No. 4, Part 2 (September 1956).

It is our further judgment that the public should be warned against faddish aspects of this movement. No new venture in American education can long prosper without the wholehearted support of parents, teachers, and educational administrators in a given community.· Proponents of foreign-language study in the elementary schools should not, therefore, initiate programs until

1. a majority of the parents concerned approve at least an experimental program, and

2. local school boards and administrators are convinced that necessary preparations have been made.

Necessary preparations include:

1. recruitment of an adequate number of interested teachers who have both skill in guiding children and the necessary language qualifications.

2. availability of material appropriate to each age level, with new approaches and a carefully planned syllabus for each grade, and

3. adequate provisions for appraisal.

The success of existing programs thus initiated, prepared for, and appraised convinces us of the urgent need of providing, for children who have the ability and desire, the opportunity for continuous progress in language study into and through junior and senior high school.

A SECOND STATEMENT OF POLICY

A. *Five Years Later.* Since the publication in 1956 of the first MLA statement on FLES, there has been increasing awareness of the need for an early start to foreign language learning. There is equal awareness of the dangers of inadequate attempts to meet this need. Hundreds of communities have ignored our warning against "faddish aspects of this movement" and our insistence upon "necessary preparations." Many of the resulting programs have been wasteful and disappointing, and they have misled many citizens about the nature and value of foreign-language learning.

B. *Redefinition.* We must sharpen our definition of FLES. It is not an end in itself but the elementary-school (K-6) part of a language-learning program that should extend unbroken through grade 12. It has 15- or 20-minute sessions at least three times a week as an integral part of the school day. It concerns itself primarily with learning the four language skills, beginning with listening and speaking. Other values (improved understanding of language in general, intercultural understanding, broadened horizons), though important, are secondary.

C. *FLES in Sequence.* We believe that FLES, as here defined, is an essential part of the long sequence, ten years or more, needed to approach mastery of a second language in school. There is good evidence that the learning of a second language considerably quickens and eases the learning of a third language, even when there is little or no relation between the languages learned. Since children imitate skillfully and with few inhibitions in the early school years, the primary grades (K-3) are the ideal place to begin language learning, and the experience is in itself exciting and rewarding.

D. *Priority.* If a school system cannot provide both a FLES program and a six-year elementary-school foreign-language sequence (grades 7-12), it should work first toward establishing the grade 7-12 sequence. Unless there is a solid junior- and senior-high-school program of foreign-language learning with due stress on the listening and speaking skills and fully articulated with the previous instruction, FLES learnings wither on the vine.

E. *Articulation.* It requires: 1) a foreign-language program in grades 7 and 8 for graduates of FLES, who should never he placed with beginners at any grade level; 2) a carefully planned coordination of the FLES and secondary-school programs; 3) a frequent interchange of visits and information among the foreign-language teachers at all levels; 4) an overall coordination by a single foreign-language supervisor or by a committee of administrators. These cooperative efforts should result in a common core of language learning that will make articulation smooth and effective.

F. *Experimental Programs.* Experimentation is desirable in education, but we now know enough about FLES methods and materials to obviate the need for "pilot" or "experimental" programs if these adjectives mean no more than "tentative" or "reluctant." If a shortage of teachers makes it impossible to offer instruction to all the pupils in a grade, a partial FLES program is an acceptable temporary expedient, but it will pose a special scheduling problem in grade 7. An "experimental" program should be a genuine experiment, not a desperate, inadequately planned program instituted by community pressure against the advice of language authorities in the field.

Experimentation in *methods* should be undertaken only after teachers and administrators are thoroughly familiar with current theories of foreign-language learning and with current practices in successful FLES programs. The development of experimental teaching *materials* should be undertaken only after teachers are thoroughly familiar with existing materials.

G. *The Teacher.* Ideally he should be an expert in the foreign language he teaches, with near-native accent and fluency, and also skillful in teaching young children. Few teachers are currently expert in both areas. If a teacher's foreign-language accent is not good, he should make every effort to improve it, and meanwhile he should rely on discs or tapes to supply authentic model voices for his pupils. But since language is communication, and a child cannot communicate with a phonograph or tape recorder, no FLES learning can be wholly successful without the regular presence in the classroom of a live model who is also an expert teacher. The shortage of such doubly skilled teachers is the most serious obstacle to the success of FLES. To relieve this shortage every institution that trains future elementary-school teachers should offer a major in one or more foreign languages.

H. *Cautions.* A FLES program should be instituted only if: 1) it is an integral and serious part of the school day; 2) it is an integral and serious part of the total foreign-language program in the school system; 3) there is close articulation with later foreign-language learning; 4) there are available FL specialists or elementary-school teachers with an adequate command of the foreign language; 5) there is a planned syllabus and a sequence of appropriate teaching materials; 6) the program has the support of the administration; 7) the high-school teachers of the foreign language in the local school system recognize the same long-range objectives and practice some of the same teaching techniques as the FLES teachers.

The need for a revised statement on FLES was the subject of a conference on 27 and 28 January 1961. Participants in this conference: Theodore Andersson, Emma Birkmaier, Nelson Brooks, Josephine Bruno, Dorothy Chamberlain, Austin E. Fife, Elton Hocking, Elizabeth Keesee, Margit W. MacRae, Kenneth W. Mildenberger, Ruth Mulhauser, William R. Parker, Filomena Peloro, Gordon R. Silber, G. Winchester Stone Jr., Mary P. Thompson, W. Freeman Twaddel, Donald D. Walsh, Helen B. Yakobson.

The statement was developed and authorized by the Advisory and Liaison Committees of the Modern Language Association, whose members are Theodore Andersson, William B. Edgerton, Austin E. Fife, John G. Kuntsmann, William R. Parker, Norman P. Sacks, Gordon R. Silber, Jack M. Stein, Louis Tenenbaum, W. Freeman Twaddell, and Helen B. Yakobson.

Bibliography

References that have been quoted in the text are not included in this bibliography. Although other languages are mentioned, this list is confined to the teaching of French in the elementary school and during the important period of transition in the junior high school. No attempt has been made to include references in the highly specialized areas of linguistics or the use of the language laboratory.

GENERAL BIBLIOGRAPHY AND RESOURCE LISTS

Birkmaier, Emma M., "Modern Languages," *Encyclopedia of Educational Research*, 3rd ed., Chester W. Harris, ed. New York: The Macmillan Company, 1960, pp. 861–88. A summary of the foreign language program in the elementary school, with emphasis on research.

Chamber of Commerce of the United States, *Guide to Foreign Information Sources*, rev. ed. Washington, D.C.: The Chamber, 1961. This booklet also contains names and addresses of organizations and services relating to different areas of the world and good bibliographical references on the United Nations, travel, and employment abroad.

The French Review, a bi-monthly publication of the American Association of Teachers of French. Available from Mr. George B. Watts, Davidson College, Davidson, N.C. Contains articles on literature, methodology, foreign language programs, descriptions of new publications, and AATF news. Of special interest is the section entitled "NIB News," which describes realia, audio-visual materials, books, and reprints of articles that are available.

Glaude, Paul M., *Selective Guide to the Acquisition of Audio-Lingual and Related Materials Useful in Teaching Foreign Languages in the "New Key."* Philadelphia: Chilton Co., 1961. Contains lists of materials and their sources for teachers of French, German, Italian, Latin, Russian, and Spanish.

Keesee, Elizabeth, *References on Foreign Languages in the Elementary School*, Office of Education Bulletin OE27008B. Washington, D.C.: U.S. Government Printing Office, 1963. Professional materials, instructional materials in six languages, and addresses of publishers and importers.

Modern Language Abstracts. Fullerton, Cal.: Department of Foreign Languages and Literature, Orange County State College, quarterly (including annual cumulative index). Bibliographical listings with short abstracts of articles and books "to keep you abreast of research and opinion relevant to the teaching of modern languages."

The Modern Language Journal. Published eight times a year by the National Federation of Modern Language Teachers Associations. Available from Mr. Stephen L. Pitcher, 7144 Washington Ave., St. Louis 30, Mo. Contains articles on literature, methodology, foreign-language programs, and descriptions of new publications.

Nostrand, Howard L., et al., *Research on Language Teaching: An Annotated Bibliography for 1945–61*. Seattle: University of Washington Press, 1962. A useful reference for all foreign-language teachers.

Ollmann, Mary J., ed., *Modern Language Association List of Materials for Use by Teachers of Modern Foreign Languages in Elementary and Secondary Schools*. New York: Modern Language Association Foreign Language Program Research Center (MLA-FLP), 1962. An annotated bibliography of books on methodology, other references for teachers, and available materials for French, German, Italian, Modern Hebrew, Norwegian, Polish, Portuguese, Russian, Spanish, and Swedish. Detailed ratings are given according to elaborate criteria that have been set up for evaluating the various categories.

Rufsvold, Margaret I. and Carolyn Guss, *Guides to Newer Educational Media*. Chicago: American Library Association, 1961. A catalogue of catalogues, periodicals, professional organizations, and selected bibliography, with descriptive annotations. Though many other subjects are included, it is invaluable to foreign-language teachers.

Service Bureau for Modern Language Teachers, Kansas State Teachers College, Emporia, Kansas. Bulletins on conversation lists, realia information, holidays, and festivals.

Van Eenenaam, Evelyn, "Annotated Bibliography of Modern Language Methodology for the Year," *Modern Language Journal* (annual, usually in the January issue). A very useful reference for foreign language teachers.

Valuable information is also available in the FLES Section of *Hispania*.

METHODOLOGY

Andersson, Theodore, *The Teaching of Foreign Languages in the Elementary School.* Boston: D. C. Heath & Company, 1953. A pioneering study by an outstanding authority.

Brooks, Nelson, *Language and Language Learning: Theory and Practice.* New York: Harcourt, Brace & World, Inc., 1960. Very good on the philosophy and methodology of modern foreign-language teaching. Valuable for the language laboratory. Good appendix, containing suggestions for classroom procedures and methods, a glossary, and a bibliography.

Dunkel, Harold B. and Roger A. Pillet, *French in the Elementary School: Five Years' Experience.* Chicago: University of Chicago Press, 1962. An account of the introduction of French into the curriculum of the University of Chicago Elementary School. This book gives an analytical description of the problems encountered in the development of the project, including planning the program, staffing and scheduling, methods and materials used, the goals attained, and articulation with the high school.

Galas, Evangeline M. and Filomena Peloro, *HRS Manual for Teachers and Parents.* Baltimore: Ottenheimer Publishers, Inc., 1960. A guide to the presentation and drill of recorded dialogue for young children.

"How the Army Teaches Foreign Languages," *School Management*, Vol. V, No. 7 (July, 1961), 44–50. Questions and answers covering the straightforward approach to foreign-language teaching.

Huebener, Theodore, *Audio-Visual Techniques in Teaching Foreign Languages.* New York: New York University Press, 1960. A practical treatment of the uses of various audio-visual materials and a presentation of laboratory procedures. Intended for teachers on all levels. Concrete examples of dramatizations given in French, German, and Spanish. A useful FLES bibliography for French and Spanish, a list of films and filmstrips for several languages, and addresses of sources of materials are included.

————, *How to Teach Foreign Languages Effectively.* New York: New York University Press, 1959. Pedagogically conservative. Helpful advice for the beginning teacher. Useful bibliographies.

Keesee, Elizabeth, *Modern Foreign Languages in the Elementary School:*

Teaching Techniques, Office of Education Bulletin OE27007, No. 29. Washington, D. C.: U.S. Government Printing Office, 1960. This bulletin describes and illustrates, in French and Spanish, techniques to be used in the classroom. It includes the teaching of dialogues, narratives, and descriptions, visual materials, games, and testing. A very useful handbook that translates familiar theory into actual practice.

Lonjaret, J. and R. Denis, *L'Enseignement précoce de l'anglais au niveau primaire élémentaire (la première année).* Paris: Institut Pédagogique National, n.d. The teacher's manual for the teaching of English in the elementary schools of France.

MacRae, Margit W., *Teaching Spanish in the Grades.* Boston: Houghton Mifflin Company, 1957. A useful reference for any FLES teacher, regardless of the language. Main emphasis is placed upon the story-telling method. It contains detailed suggestions on guides, materials, and procedure. There are accompanying records and pupil notebooks.

Méras, Edmond A., *A Language Teacher's Guide,* rev. ed. New York: Harper & Row, Publishers, 1962. Aims at helping language teachers solve problems by recommending a number of techniques and their proper application. A series of daily lessons for presenting French to an elementary class.

O'Connor, Patricia, *Modern Foreign Languages in High School: Pre-Reading Instruction,* Office of Education Bulletin OE27000, No. 9. Washington, D. C.: U.S. Government Printing Office, 1960. Presents the theory of aural-oral foundation in language teaching, with examples. Transition to reading is explained. Useful for teachers on all levels.

FLES MANUALS IN FRENCH

Kolbert, Jack and Harry Goldby, *First (and Second) French Handbook(s) for Teachers in Elementary Schools.* Pittsburgh: University of Pittsburgh Press, 1958, 1960. Teacher's manuals developed primarily for the regular classroom teacher who conducts a French program under the guidance of a language specialist.

Modern Language Association of America, *MLA Teacher's Guide: Beginning French in Grade Three,* rev. ed. Darien, Conn.: Teachers Publishing Corporation, 1959. One twelve-inch LP disc included. Course guide to conversational French. No specific tests or means of evaluating pupil progress, but otherwise an excellent course containing interesting dialogues.

_____, *MLA Teacher's Guide: French in Grade Four,* rev. ed. Darien, Conn.: Teachers Publishing Corporation, 1963. Units, songs, games, materials on objectives, references and instructions for the teacher. Record is available.

_____, *MLA Teacher's Guide: French in Grade Five.* Darien, Conn.:

Teachers Publishing Corporation, 1963. A good course guide for teachers of French.

Raymond, M. and Claude L. Bourcier, (1) *Bonjour*, (2) *Venez voir*, (3) *Je sais lire*, (4) *Je lis avec joie*, Elementary French Series. Boston: Allyn and Bacon, Inc., 1959, 1960. Attractive pictures supply the subject matter for oral teaching in Books 1 and 2. Reading is presented in Books 3 and 4. The teacher's edition provides many suggestions. Recordings are also available.

FLES REFERENCES FOR THE TEACHER AND ADMINISTRATOR

Audiovisual Instruction, Vol. VII, No. 9 (November, 1962). Contains excellent articles on the 1959 issue of *Audiovisual Instruction*, teacher education, FLES, testing, the Peace Corps, and a selective bibliography on language teaching and AV. This issue is devoted entirely to foreign-language instruction.

California State Department of Education, *French for Listening, Speaking, Reading, Writing*. Sacramento: The Department, 1962. Vol. XXXI, No. 4. A handbook for language instructors and other school personnel of the state. Objectives, basic principles, evaluation, and audio-visual materials are discussed in terms of a six- or seven-year sequence, including junior and senior high school.

———, *Looking Ahead in Foreign Languages*. Sacramento: The Department, 1961. The importance of understanding the nature of language learning, the purposes of FLES, when to begin, and criteria for selecting the language to be taught are discussed by national leaders in the field. Good survey of views on major FLES problems.

———, *Reports of Regional Conferences on Improving Modern Foreign Languages in Elementary Schools*. Sacramento: The Department, 1962. Summaries of discussions and papers read at two regional conferences. Sample materials used in the workshops are included.

Childers, J. Wesley, Donald D. Walsh, and G. Winchester Stone, Jr., eds., *Reports of Surveys and Studies in the Teaching of Modern Foreign Languages*. New York: MLA-FLP, 1961. Reports of twenty-one surveys and studies made in 1959–61. Articles on FLES and high school practices. Very valuable for teachers and administrators.

"Dr. Conant Looks at the Junior High School," *National Parent Teacher*, Vol. 54, No. 9 (May, 1960), 4, 5, 6, 35. A tentative report on the organization and curriculum of the junior high school. Includes a brief, objective discussion of the longer sequence of foreign-language study and the important administrative role played by the principal in the articulation between junior and senior high school. A recommended reference for junior high personnel.

Gradisnik, Anthony, and Robert Suchy, *El Español en las Escuelas Pri-*

marias: *Report on a Trial Program in New Approaches to the Teaching of Spanish at the Fifth and Sixth Grade Levels, with Instructional Television as the Major Resource.* Milwaukee: Milwaukee Public Schools, 1962. An attractively printed booklet on evaluating a FLES program. Both the program and the tests used to evaluate it are described.

Huebener, Theodore, *Why Johnny Should Learn Foreign Languages.* Philadelphia: Chilton Co., 1961. A good book for the layman or the school library and an excellent reference for foreign-language teachers. A brief history of foreign languages in the United States and a sketch of the chief languages throughout the world are given. Vocational needs for fluency in a foreign language are stressed, especially in the fields of international relations, business, and military defense.

Johnston, Marjorie C., "The Foreign Language Teacher at Work," *School Life,* Vol. XLIV, No. 9 (1962), 18. An article that includes concrete, well-illustrated examples of the use of modern audio-visual aids on all levels throughout the country.

Massachusetts Council for Public Schools, *FLES: Foreign Languages in Elementary Schools, A Study of Teaching Foreign Languages to Young Children by the Oral Method.* Boston: The Council, 1957. A pamphlet or study of the early days of the FLES movement which includes discussions of the direct method, foreign language and the elementary school curriculum, and descriptions of elementary French programs in Medford, Dracut, and Andover, Mass.

Metropolitan School Study Council, *Some Solutions to Problems Related to the Teaching of Foreign Languages in Elementary Schools.* New York: The Council, 1956. This report was written by the Committee on Foreign Languages in the Elementary Schools appointed by the Metropolitan School Study Council. It contains some definite suggestions for putting a program of teaching foreign languages below grade eight into operation.

MLA Cooperative Foreign Language Tests, prepared under the direction of Nelson Brooks. Princeton, N.J.: Educational Testing Service, 1963. Both batteries test the four language skills in French, German, Italian, Russian, and Spanish. Norms will be established for classes from junior high school through the sophomore year in college.

MLA Proficiency Tests for Teachers and Advanced Students, prepared under the direction of Wilmarth Starr. Princeton, N.J.: Educational Testing Service, 1962. These tests are being used in some states for certification of teachers, by some colleges as part of the general examination of foreign language majors, and by some graduate schools for the evaluation of the proficiency of entering students.

Modern Language Association, *FLES Packet.* New York: MLA-FLP, 1960. An indispensable collection of sixteen documents, including trends and policy statements on the teaching of foreign languages in the elementary school, announcements of materials for teachers, the

Keesee bulletin on teaching techniques, and reprints of reports from the Northeast Conferences of 1956, 1958, and 1959.

————, *Foreign Language Discussion Pamphlets*. New York: MLA-FLP, 1959. Eight pamphlets designed for use by civic and cultural organizations in informal discussions.

National Education Association, *Foreign Languages in the Elementary School*, a special issue of *The National Elementary Principal*, Vol. XXXIX, No. 6 (1960). Issue includes seven articles on such topics as audio-visual aids in teaching foreign languages, use of television, and administration of a FLES program. It affords the reader a sample of the views expressed to elementary school principals through their professional organization.

————, "Foreign Languages in the Elementary School: A Symposium," *NEA Journal*, Vol. XLIX, No. 2 (February, 1960), 33–36. Six educators respond to the question, "What effect does FLES have on later language learning?" Evidence obtained in foreign-language programs in the University of Chicago Elementary School, Western Reserve University (FLES Institute), San Diego, Calif., and Hackensack, N.J. is cited and the national foreign language situation is summarized.

————, *The Teaching of Foreign Languages*, a special issue of the *NEA Journal*, Vol. L, No. 9 (December, 1961). Issue includes articles on junior and senior high school programs and the use of skits and games in teaching foreign languages.

REPORTS OF THE NORTHWEST CONFERENCES ON THE TEACHING OF FOREIGN LANGUAGES

Bishop, G. Reginald, Jr., ed., *Culture in Language Learning*. New Brunswick, N.J.: Department of Romance Languages, Rutgers University, 1960.

Eaton, Margaret, *The Foreign Language Program, Grades 3–12*. New York: MLA, 1958.

Peloro, Filomena, *Elementary and Junior High School Curricula*. New York: MLA, 1959.

Reports of the Working Committees, 1954–58. New Haven, Conn.: MAT Program, Yale University, 1959.

Selvi, Arthur M. and Committee, *Foreign Language Instruction in Elementary Schools*. New Haven, Conn.: MAT Program, Yale University, 1954.

Thompson, Mary P. and Committee, *Foreign Language Instruction in Elementary Schools*. Oxford, Ohio: American Classical League, Miami University, 1956.

Ohio State Department of Education, *Modern Foreign Language in Ohio Elementary Schools*. Columbus, Ohio: The Department, 1962. Brief discussions of major topics such as trends, techniques, evaluation, audio-visual aids, and suggestions as to how to initiate and administer a program.

Parker, William R., *The National Interest and Foreign Languages*, 3rd ed. Washington, D.C.: U.S. Government Printing Office, 1962. The most authoritative survey of foreign-language activity in the United States. Discussion of practical questions faced by individual communities and by the nation as a whole.

Pei, Marjorie L, et. al., *Language Structure at FLES Level*. Available from the National Information Bureau of the AATF, Brooklyn College, Brooklyn 19, N.Y. Mimeographed, 1962. A discussion of techniques for teaching structure including a section on "Testing for Mastery of Structures," prepared by the FLES Committee of the American Association of Teachers of French.

Starr, Wilmarth H., Mary P. Thompson, and Donald D. Walsh, eds., *Modern Foreign Languages and the Academically Talented Student*. New York: MLA-FLP, 1960. An especially important document, the first in this field to be produced jointly by the NEA and the MLA. It proposes the expansion of language offerings with four years as a minimum and ten years as the ideal. Stresses the importance of acquiring knowledge of other cultures as well as languages. Considers teacher qualifications and administrative problems. This document should be of interest to all teachers of foreign-language students.

Thompson, Elizabeth E. and Arthur E. Hamalainen, *Foreign Language Teaching in Elementary Schools*. Washington, D.C.: Association for Supervision and Curriculum Development, 1958. An examination of current practices. A discussion of problems arising in planning and initiating a foreign-language program, ways of achieving continuity, and methods of facilitating foreign-language teaching in elementary schools.

Walsh, Donald D., *What's What: A List of Useful Terms for the Teacher of Modern Languages*. New York: MLA-FLP, 1963. A glossary of new terms used in foreign-language teaching. Cross references and a short bibliography are given.

BASIC TEXTS FOR PUPILS (GRADES 6, 7, and 8)

De Sauzé, Emile B., *Nouveau cours pratique de français pour commençants*. New York: Holt, Rinehart & Winston, Inc., 1959. Written for the first two years of junior high school or the first year of senior high school. All material is in French including the grammar. Reading passages are in the form of dialogues. Supplementary materials are also available.

De Sauzé, Emile B. and Agnès M. Dureau, *Un Peu de tout: Second French Reader*, revised by Eugene K. Dawson. New York: Holt, Rinehart & Winston, Inc., 1951. Designed to follow the *Nouveau cours pratique*. Material is carefully graded and provides a cultural background.

Ernst, Frédéric and Sylvia N. Levy, *Le Français*, Books I–II. New York: Holt, Rinehart & Winston, Inc., 1959. The twenty preliminary lessons serve as a transition from elementary to junior high school French, as most of the material is taught in elementary courses. Each of the chapters contains one point of grammar and text in the form of a conversation and exercises. Cultural material is included in both books.

Harris, Julian and Hélène Monod-Cassidy, *Petites Conversations*. Boston: D. C. Heath & Company, 1956. The lessons are composed of dialogues suitable for upper elementary grades. Songs, games, readings on culture, and fables of La Fontaine are included. Disc available.

————, *Nouvelles Conversations*. Boston: D. C. Heath & Company, 1961. Second book in the series and suitable for junior high school, as some grammar is taught. Much oral drill and many exercises and dialogues are given. Delightfully illustrated. Disc and tapes available.

————, *Conversations d'aujourd'hui*. Boston: D. C. Heath & Company, 1962. Third book in the series and more advanced. It introduces cultural readings, poems, stories, and songs. Good illustrations. Grammar is reinforced by pattern drills and exercises.

Huebener, Theodore and Marie K. Neuschatz, *Parlez-vous français?* Boston: D. C. Heath & Company, 1958. Twelve introductory lessons. Conversation, reading, and grammar are combined in the lessons that follow. This book is followed by *Oui, je parle français* (Boston: D. C. Heath & Company, 1958).

Mauger, G. and G. Gougenheim, *Le Français Elémentaire*, 2 vols. Paris: Librairie Hachette, 1955, 1956. Three LP discs for each volume. Useful books for junior high school. Many pictures illustrate basic structural patterns in daily conversation. A set of twelve charts (twenty-four pictures) designed for use with these texts is also available.

Pei, Marjorie L., *J'étudie le français à la maison et à l'école*. St. Louis: Gelles-Widmer Co., 1960. Attractively illustrated, direct-method workbook. A good introduction to reading, with conversational practice for upper elementary grades.

Vogt, Vivian T., *Suzanne et Pierre*. Lexington, Mass.: privately published by author (8 Foster Road) 1963. A first reading book for pupils who have had oral French. Material is suitable to the age, interest, and language background of students in grades 5 and 6. Special edition available for teachers.

INTEGRATED PROGRAMS

A-LM Program. New York: Harcourt, Brace & World, Inc., 1961, 1962, 1963. These materials consist of four levels of learning. Level One represents a typical year's work of five forty-five-minute periods a week. Through use of the Audio-Lingual Materials, pupils learn to pronounce the phrases and sentences without reference to the written word. The student is introduced to the foreign language via everyday situations, which are presented in dialogue form. In this way, the sound of the language becomes familiar to the student before he sees the written language. Skills of reading and writing are developed after a beginning has been made in the development of listening and speaking skills. These materials include a student text, teacher's manual, classroom or laboratory tapes, and student practice records. Levels Two and Three show a gradual transition from emphasis on the spoken language to emphasis on reading. Level Four will be published in late 1964.

Cornfield, Ruth R., *French for Beginners*. New York: Teaching Audials and Visuals, Inc., 1962. A set of six audio-visual-lingual teaching units for use in the elementary school: "La Salle de classe." "A l'école," "Ma famille," "Ma maison," "Ma petite ville," and "Aux Tuileries." Each packet consists of a record, filmstrip, wall chart, pin-pointer for locating specific material on the record, and teacher's manual.

Coté, Dominique G., Sylvia N. Levy, and Patricia O'Connor, *Ecouter et parler*. New York: Holt, Rinehart & Winston, Inc., 1962. A beginning French course for secondary pupils, seventh through ninth grades. The course consists of a student's book, a teacher's edition, set of sixty flashcards in color, workbook, grading chart, testing program, practice records, and complete tape recordings. The text is in accord with the latest language goals and principles of language learning. Second- and third-year courses are in preparation. The second- and third-year books are: *Parler et lire*, 1963, and *Parler, lire et écrire*, 1964.

Evans, James A. and Marie Baldwin, *Learning French the Modern Way*. New York: McGraw-Hill Book Company, Inc., 1961, 1963, Book I and Book II. Each level includes one book, filmstrips, four motion pictures, tape recordings, three reels of taped tests and printed test booklets.

Guberina, P. and P. Rivenc, *Voix et images de France*. Philadelphia: Chilton Co., 1962. *Cours préliminaire* is for Grades 4, 5, and 6; *Premier Degré* for Grades 7–8; *Deuxième Degré* for Grades 9–10. Filmstrips, tapes, teacher texts, guides, and laboratory tapes are provided for the teacher; take-home records, reading texts, and workbooks for the student. These materials grew out of studies made by the Commission de Français Fondamental and were developed by the Centre de Recherche et d'Etude pour la Diffusion du Francais at the Ecole Normale Supérieure de Saint-Cloud.

Pathescope-Berlitz Audio-Visual French Language Series. New York: Pathescope Educational Films, Inc., 1959. Eight sets of five lessons each to be used as supplements to basic courses. Graded for a two- or three-year sequence. Each set consists of five 35mm color filmstrips made in France, recordings of dialogue by native speakers, and a teacher's guide. Two reels of listening comprehension tests are also available for the series. For junior and senior high school.

Rosselot, LaVelle, *Je parle français*. Wilmette, Ill.: Encyclopaedia Britannica Films, 1961. A three-year program composed of 120 film lessons and 120 five-inch tapes. A well-integrated basic course using films, texts, and tapes suitable for junior or senior high school. Interesting and colorful films should do much to motivate students. Many people from various parts of France participate in the conversations.

Slack, Anne, *Parlons français*. Boston: Heath de Rochemont Corporation, 1960. A complete course for teaching French in the elementary school. Available in television and film versions, each with aids for guiding classroom follow-up. The program for the first year consists of: (1) basic television or film lessons taught by Mme Slack, a native French teacher; (2) supplementary audio-visual materials, including motion pictures for teacher preparation and plastic records for pupil practice; (3) audio-lingual activity books for pupils; and (4) teacher's guides with detailed instructions. The films, depicting family life in France, are the basis of the fifteen-minute lessons. *Parlons français* was first produced by the Modern Language Project of the Massachusetts Council for Public Schools. This integrated program would be especially useful in large school systems having few qualified teachers.

SONGS AND RECORDS

Les Albums de l'Oncle Max, FQ 8004. New York: Folkways Records and Service Corp. Book 1, *Nos amis, les animaux*; Book 2, *Jeannot Lapin*; Book 3, *Paul et Paulette*. Two ten-inch LP records with booklets by Frances H. Patterson.

Children of Paris, LP-GA 33-ORG-501. Harrison, N.J.: Grand Award Record Corp. The teaching of French songs is aided by the use of this record. The fact that the songs are sung by both French and American children helps to develop a feeling of brotherhood across the sea.

A Child's Introduction to French. New York: Golden Records. One ten-inch LP disc with text. Lessons by Pearl S. Bennet. French instruction under the direction of Dr. Bernard Blau. Distributed by Affiliated Publishers, Inc., Rockefeller Center, New York, N.Y.

Cornfield, Ruth R., *The Song Game Lessons*. New York: Teaching Audials and Visuals, Inc. Fr. 601: "Les amis," on numbers; "Je vais à Paris," on modes of transportation; Fr. 602: "Les animaux," on animals; "Bonjour, mademoiselle," on parts of the body. Each unit consists of a filmstrip and teaching tapes through which the basic lessons are given with music and words of the songs. A teacher's manual contains additional games.

De Cesare, Ruth, *Chansons pour la classe de français*. New York: Mills Music, Inc., and Los Angeles: Curriculum Materials Center. Book and record for any level, containing familiar French folk songs with music. Instructions for group activities appropriate for secondary pupils.

Eddy, Frederick D., et al., *French for Children*. Baltimore: Ottenheimer Publishers, Inc. An album of the HRS ("Hear-Repeat-Speak") Language Course for Children. This record may be played in the classroom if the proper preparation and follow-up activities are offered. The discussion after each section should be in French. There are twelve units, each consisting of a dialogue by children about everyday objects and situations, such as pets and family life. Illustrated booklet included. (See also Galas in the section on methodology, p. 164.)

Fables de La Fontaine, No. 1. A Pergola recording. New York: The French Book Guild. Fables include: "Le renard et la cigogne," "Le loup et l'agneau," "Le loup et le chien," and "Le corbeau et le renard."

French Children's Songs for Teaching French, FP 8003. A Phonotapes, Inc. recording. New York: Folkways Records & Service Corp. Twenty-two songs with text in English and French.

French for the Younger Set. New York: University Associated Children's Educational Records. An album of teaching records for children aged three to eight. Fun in French and English with simple, captivating songs, games, and activities. Planned to entertain and to stimulate the child's natural ability to learn new sounds and words.

Gessler, Elizabeth F., *Chantons* and *Chantons encore*. New York: Gessler Publishing Co., 1960, 1962. Small paperback songbooks that may be used in the elementary school. The second volume has notes and directions for games and dramatizations.

House, Marguerite, *Here We Come A-Caroling: Christmas Carols Arranged for Two-Part Treble Voices*. Minneapolis: Hall & McCreary Company, 1954. This collection includes two French carols: "Sommeil de l'Enfant Jésus" and "La Marche des rois."

Jacob, Suzanne, *Children's Living French Records*. New York: Lothrop, Lee & Shepard Co., Inc., 1960. Two ten-inch LP records, conversational manual and dictionary.

Let's Sing Songs in French, Cabot 4101. Baltimore: Ottenheimer Publishers, Inc. One twelve-inch LP disc with accompanying text and music. This is a fine recording, which presents an excellent model of eight popular songs for children. A man and a woman alternate in singing and teaching the songs. This record is particularly helpful because of clear articulation, since the lines are spoken as well as sung and pupils can learn the verses without help from a teacher.

Mon Premier Livre de chansons. Paris: Librairie Larousse, 1959. With discs. Illustrated by Hélène Poirié. Contains "Trois Jeunes Tambours," a very popular song with adolescents.

Noëls. A Pergola recording. New York: The French Book Guild. A 45 RPM record and illustrated booklet with text and music. The carols included are: "Mon Beau Sapin," "Belle Nuit, sainte nuit," "Entre le boeuf et l'âne gris," and "Les Anges dans nos campagnes."

On Location France, DL 9086. New York: Decca Records, Inc. Record of music, voices, and sounds of Paris and festivals of France with eight pages of English commentary.

Le Petit Colleur d'affiches. Narrated by Daniel Dorian. Collection

Capucine. Paris: Fernand Nathan. A tape recording of a lovely children's tale adapted for adults and children.

Rondes No. 7. A Pergola recording. New York: The French Book Guild. A 45 RPM record and illustrated booklet with text and music. It includes "J'ai perdu le do" and "Promenons-nous dans les bois."

Van de Velde, Ernest, *Chantons, dansons.* Tours, France: Maison Mame, 1936. Music, verses, and beautiful illustrations for some of the familiar folk songs, as well as for several that are not so well known.

Vigneras, Marcel, *Chansons de France,* rev. ed. Boston: D. C. Heath & Company, 1962. A collection of songs that may be used by pupils in sixth grade through secondary school. Contains piano accompaniments and aids to pronunciation.

FILMS, FILMSTRIPS, AND SLIDES

Bim. 1950. A movie available at FACSEA (see addresses). Catalogue No. 404. A children's adventure story with an Arab setting. A little boy loses his beloved donkey to the Caïd's son, eventually retrieving it after many adventures. Text by Jacques Prévert and Albert Lamorisse. Available in book form, illustrated with cuts from the film. (See Library Books, p. 177.)

A Colorslide Tour of France. New York: Columbia Record Club. A book with colored slides and projector.

Crin Blanc. 1952. A movie available at FACSEA. Catalogue No. 400. Filmed in France by Albert Lamorisse. The story of a white horse of the Camargue that refuses to be tamed by anyone until he meets Folco, a young boy. They become friends as Folco helps him escape from the cowboys who are trying to capture him. (See Library Books, p. 177.)

En Bretagne, Fr. 201; *A la plage,* Fr. 202; *Paris—La Ville pour flâner,* Fr. 203; *La douce France,* Fr. 204; *Du Haut de Notre Dame de Paris,* Fr. 205; *Tout Droit au Sacré-Coeur,* Fr. 206. New York: Teaching Audials and Visuals Inc., 1960. Each unit consists of a filmstrip and an LP record prepared for junior high school pupils. Aural comprehension and dictation exercises.

La Famille française Brunel. New York: McGraw-Hill Book Company, Inc. A 16mm black and white sound film made in Blois, available in both French and English. An enlightening visit to the home of a French family as related by a thirteen-year-old girl. The film may also be rented from educational film libraries.

Une Fête foraine à Paris. Available at FACSEA. Catalogue No. KA50. A set of kodachrome slides and accompanying text. A street fair in the square near *Les Invalides* is described from the point of view of an eleven-year-old.

French for Elementary Schools. New York: Young America Filmstrips, McGraw-Hill Book Company, Inc. Set 1: "La Famille Dupont," "La

Salle de classe," "La Leçon de mathématique," "Le Magasin," "Michel est malade," "La Fête de l'anniversaire." Set 2: "Les Parents de Michel," "La Maison," "La Journée de Michel," "L'Epicerie libre service," "Les Amis de Michel," "La Ferme." Each set contains six color filmstrips and three LP records with a teacher's manual. The filmstrips dramatize stories of everyday activities of American children. The stories are told in simple French, then repeated with French captions on each frame.

Paris, Filme Fixe No. 1524. Paris: Editafilms. Other color filmstrips produced by Editafilms are: No. 1858, *Un Bon Dimanche*; No. 1886, *Les Joies de la neige*; No. 1525. *Un Grand Port: Marseille*; No. 822, *Le Vilain petit canard*; No. 824, *La Petite Fille aux alumettes*; No. 1878, *Un Voyage en paquebot*; No. 1822, *La Flute enchantée*; No. 1860, *La Ferme*; and No. 1897, *Le Cirque*. These attractive filmstrips were planned for young children, but many of them may be used through eighth grade. A simple, written commentary is included with each film but is not on the strip itself.

Pillet, Roger, *En Classe*. Chicago: Coronet Films. A one-year course composed of twenty color filmstrips with accompanying recordings, teacher's manual, and a special record for the teacher. It has been planned for use in third grade by a French specialist or by a classroom teacher who has some knowledge of French. Familiar material is reviewed. These lessons center around the classroom.

Les Santons—Noël. A set of forty slides available at FACSEA. Catalogue No. SA 56. The story of Christmas is told by means of the little figures of the santons of Provence.

La Seine, Paris: Le Centre National Pédagogique. A film available at FACSEA. Catalogue No. 753. A teaching film showing the course of the Seine River from its source down to Le Havre. Aimed at elementary schools, but a very old film and with very slow commentary.

(For other films, filmstrips, and slides see the FACSEA catalogue)

LIBRARY BOOKS FOR BOYS AND GIRLS

Bemelmans, Ludwig, *Madeline's Rescue*. New York: The Viking Press, Inc. 1953. Madeline falls into the Seine and is rescued by her dog. Grades 3–5.

Berlitz, *French for Children: The Three Bears and Little Red Riding Hood*. New York: Grosset & Dunlap, Inc., 1959. An attractive, well-illustrated book in both English and French. Grades 4–6.

Bishop, Claire H., *All Alone*. New York: The Viking Press, Inc., 1953. The experiences of ten-year-old Marcel and a friend, Pierre, as they herd their families' cows in the French Alps. Grades 5–6.

———, *The Big Loop*. New York: The Viking Press, Inc., 1955. This book describes the Tour de France, the famous bicycle race. Grades 5–7.

Bishop, Claire H., *Pancakes—Paris.* New York: The Viking Press, Inc., 1947. A story of World War II. A French boy finds a box of pancake mix bearing English directions. After many efforts to secure help in reading the directions, he finds two American soldiers who come home with him and help him prepare a meal for the family. Grades 5–7.

———, *Twenty and Ten.* New York: The Viking Press, Inc., 1952. A nun takes French children to the mountains, where they hide refugee children. A tale of courage and kindness. Grades 5–7.

Bragdon, Lillian F., *It's Fun to Speak French.* Nashville, Tenn.: Abingdon Press, 1962. How FLES came to Mary's room in school. Attractive drawings. A pronunciation guide and an English-French vocabulary are given. Also included are songs, a simplified version of "La Chèvre de Monsieur Seguin," "Le Corbeau et le renard" in the original and with an English translation, and a few exercises for vocabularly building. Grades 4–6.

Brown, Marcia, *Une drôle de soupe.* New York: Charles Scribner's Sons, 1960. This amusing story from Brittany, entitled *Stone Soup* in English, recounts an adventure of three hungry soldiers. For any grade.

Clément, Marguerite, *In France.* New York: The Viking Press, Inc., 1956. "An introduction to France by an author who loves the country and knows it well in all its aspects. She takes the reader to Paris and the provinces, to cathedrals and factories, to schools and homes, and shares with him some of the problems as well as the games and festivities of the people." Grades 7–9.

Cooney, Barbara, *The Little Juggler.* New York: Hastings House, Publishers, Inc., 1961. A short story in text and pictures about the little juggler, Barnaby, whose humble Christmas gift was so graciously received by the Virgin Mary. Appropriate for middle-elementary pupils.

Diska, Pat and Chris Jenkyns, *Andy Says Bonjour!* New York: Vanguard Press, 1954. An American boy sees Paris with his friend Minou, the cat. A simple story with charming pictures for children through the fourth grade.

Dupré, Ramona, *Trop de Chiens.* Chicago: Follett Publishing Company, 1960. One LP record accompanies the text. An interesting dog story for young children. May also be used as a beginning reader.

Françoise, *Minou.* New York: Charles Scribner's Sons, 1962. Nénette, a little girl in Paris, has lost her white cat. She looks for him everywhere—in a bookshop, a hatshop, a café, a restaurant; she even asks the woman who sells fish and the man who sweeps the street. A charming, colorful picture story for young children.

———, *Noël for Jeanne-Marie.* New York: Charles Scribner's Sons, 1953. A charming story about Jeanne-Marie and her pet sheep, Patapon, who live on a farm in the south of France. Jeanne-Marie talks to her pet about Father Noël but does not expect to receive anything from him. Beautiful illustrations. May be read with ease by children in third and fourth grades.

Gottlieb, Gerald, *The First Book of France,* illustrated by Alan Moyler.

New York: Franklin Watts, Inc., 1959. The author describes French life. He tells of family life, schools, sports, holidays, Paris, the châteaux of the Loire, the prehistoric cave paintings of the Dordogne, and many other historic and beautiful places in France. Grades 4–7.

Guillot, René, *The Wild, White Stallion*. New York: Franklin Watts, Inc., 1961. Based upon the story of Folco and White Mane in the setting of the mysterious and beautiful Camargue. Lovely illustrations. Grades 4–6.

Hameau, Marie-Anne, *Je lis; tu lis*. Paris: Librairie Hachette, 1960. A reference book for pupils who are learning to read. A large number of attractive pictures illustrating words and sentences common to many elementary courses.

Holl, Adelaïde, *Lisette*. New York: Lothrop, Lee & Shepard Co., Inc., 1962. The French poodle Lisette, who is a photographer's model in Paris, comes to Hollywood expecting fame and fortune. The first part of the story describes life in Paris and Lisette's trip on the Liberté. A delightful picture story. Grades 3–6.

Janice, *Angélique*. New York: McGraw-Hill Book Company, Inc., 1960. Angélique was the happiest duck in Paris until a little black poodle came along. For young children.

Joslin, Sesyle, *There Is a Dragon in My Bed; Il y a un dragon dans mon lit*. New York: Harcourt, Brace & World, Inc., 1961. A delightful book containing many expressions taught in elementary French classes. The amusing antics of a boy and girl taking a trip to Paris are described in simple sentences accompanied by humorous illustrations. In both English and French. A pronunciation guide is provided.

Lamorisse, Albert et Jacques Prévert, *Bim, le petit âne*. Paris: Librairie Hachette, 1952. A children's adventure story with an Arab setting. Abdallah, a little boy, loses his beloved donkey to the Caid's son and to robbers, eventually retrieving it after many adventures. Large, attractive photographs from the film. Grades 4–6. (See p. 174.)

———, et D. Colomb de Daunant, *Crin Blanc*, Paris: Librairie Hachette, 1953. The story of the prize-winning film, *Crin Blanc*, is told. A white horse of the Camargue refuses to be tamed by anyone until he meets Folco, a young boy. They become friends as Folco helps him escape from the cowboys who are trying to capture him. Contains large, attractive photographs from the film. Grades 4–6. (See p. 174.)

———, *The Red Balloon*. New York: Doubleday & Company, Inc., 1956. A delightful fantasy depicting the Parisian adventures of a small boy and his balloon. Appropriate for middle elementary grades.

———, *A Trip in a Balloon*. New York: Doubleday & Company. Inc., 1961. A highly imaginative picture book based upon the prize-winning film *Le Voyage en ballon*. Grades 3–5.

———, *White Mane*. New York: E. P. Dutton & Co., Inc., 1954. English translation of the text of *Crin Blanc*. Grades 5–6.

Lownsberry, Eloise, *Boy Knight of Rheims*. Boston: Houghton Mifflin Company, 1927. "The story of Jean d'Orbals, of a family of master-workmen, all of whom had helped in the building of the great cathedral of Rheims." His opportunity to contribute something comes when he is commissioned to make a statue of Jeanne d'Arc. A vivid picture of fifteenth-century Rheims. Grades 5–9.

Marokvia, Mireille, *Jannot: A French Rabbit.* Philadelphia: J. B. Lippincott Co., 1959. Jannot runs away, much to the distress of the children and neighbors. An introduction to the social structure of a small French village.

Maurois, André, *The French Boy.* New York: Sterling Publishing Company, Inc., 1957. Life in a suburban area as it is lived by Nico, a young French boy whose love for dogs and play interferes with his school work. However, he takes his studies more seriously when parental pressure is applied. Many black and white photographs. Through Grade 5.

Octave, Hélène, *A French Book to Read All by Yourself.* Boston: Little, Brown & Co., 1940. A beginning reader for those who have had at least a year of oral French.

Patterson, Lillie, *Meet Miss Liberty.* New York: The Macmillan Company, 1962. The entire story of the gift of the Statue of Liberty by the French to the American people. Bartholdi's trip to America and the inspiration he gained there, his work and Eiffel's contribution to the project are described. Colorful and interesting. Historical engravings are included. Grades 6 and up.

Reeves, Eleanor C., *Un Voyage en bateau.* Boston: Ginn & Company, 1961. André and his stowaway pets, Minou, a cat, and Princesse, a dog, take a boat trip. The provinces are introduced with their costumes and location. Gay, colorful illustrations. A delightful story for elementary pupils.

Rider, Alex, *Chez Nous.* New York: Doubleday & Company, Inc., 1961. A reader for children up to ten years of age. Illustrated by Isadore Seltzer.

———, *A la Ferme.* New York: Doubleday & Company, Inc. 1961. A reader for children up to ten years of age. Illustrated by Paul Davis.

Ross, Nancy W., *Joan of Arc.* New York: Random House, 1953. The story of the Maid of Orleans is very simply told. Grades 5–7.

Sasek, Miroslav, *This Is Paris.* New York: The Macmillan Company, 1959. A fine introduction to Paris for children of elementary school age. Contains interesting illustrations of people, famous buildings, public gardens, sidewalk cafés, and the banks of the Seine.

Sechrist, Elizabeth H. and Janette Woolsey, *It's Time for Brotherhood.* Philadelphia: Macrae Smith Co., 1962. An inspiring book containing stories of such men as Albert Schweitzer, Dag Hammarskjold, and the Four Chaplains, and of such organizations as the Red Cross, the Salvation Army, S.S. HOPE, UNICEF, the Peace Corps, and the Bilingual World. Grades 6 and up.

Selz, Irma, *Cat Sank! French for Fun.* New York: Lothrop, Lee & Shepard Co., Inc., 1961. An enjoyable book for beginning French pupils. It contains humorous drawings and references to counting, seasons, colors, family, policemen, and other simple vocabulary.

Seymour, Alta H., *The Christmas Donkey*. Chicago: Follett Publishing Company, 1953. The delightful story of a boy who has very little money and wants to get a donkey for his grandmother for Christmas. The setting is southern France. Grades 4–6.

Vacheron, Edith and Virginia Kahl, *Voici Henri!* New York: Charles Scribner's Sons, 1959. The story of a French boy and his cat is told in the simple language of most elementary French courses. Much repetition of basic patterns. Well illustrated. The same story is also available in English. Through Grade 4.

Wallace, John A., *Getting to Know France*. Eau Claire, Wis.: E. M. Hale & Company, 1962. A trip from the spires of Saint Michel in Brittany by way of Paris to Carcassonne. The reader becomes acquainted with the French people as he travels over the less familiar roads of France. Grades 3–7.

SUPPLEMENTARY MATERIALS

Caputo, Natha, *Roule galette*. Les Albums du Père Castor. Paris: Flammarion, 1950. Delightfully illustrated story for the teacher to tell the children. Pupils up to the fourth grade will recognize and appreciate this story told in simple, basic French.

Creed, Virginia, *Life in Europe: France*. Grand Rapids, Mich.: Fideler Company, 1956. A set of 8 x 11 black and white photographs and a filmstrip accompany the book, which is a suitable reference for sixth grade. The text explains all phases of modern life in France by means of a tour of the country. Illustrated with many pictures. A brief commentary may be recorded on tape to accompany the showing of the filmstrip.

Deletaille, Albertine, *Toutes Petites Histoires*. Les Albums du Père Castor. Paris: Flammarion, 1961. Very simple but charming stories about a little boat, the family, the sea, weather, and several animals that may be told to elementary school children. Basic vocabulary and lovely illustrations.

Dennison Nutrition Kit. Framingham, Mass.: Dennison Manufacturing Co. Flannel visual aids of realistic food cut-outs.

Education in France. Washington, D.C.: Editions France Actuelle, 1956. A very informative pamphlet containing a description of the structure of the educational system in France, curricula and standards, teaching methods, roles of the teacher and student, changes in educational methods, and problems confronting educators. (Two supplementary articles on educational development appeared in *France Actuelle* August 1, 1958, and June 15, 1959.)

Flannel Board Visual Aids. Philadelphia: Instructo Products Co. Foreign Language No. 306, "Farm Animals"; No. 301, "The Family"; No. 302. "The Classroom"; No. 303, "The House"; No. 304, "Christmas"; No. 305, "Parts of the Body." A word of caution is offered for those who would use materials of this kind. The teacher is advised to teach basic constructions and to use the noun pictures as a mental peg upon which to hang the entire sentence. Thus the pupils should tell a story about a picture instead of identifying objects and telling their color. Kindergarten–Grade 8.

"FLES Workshop," *The Instructor.* Dansville, N.Y.: F.A. Owen Publishing Company. A page of suggested activities, stories, games and material for elementary teachers of French and Spanish written under the direction of Miss Elizabeth Keesee, foreign language specialist in the U. S. Office of Education, is included in every issue of this magazine.

The Grade Teacher. Darien, Conn.: Teachers Publishing Corporation. A magazine for elementary school teachers published September through June. A Spanish or French play is in every issue.

Frank, J., *Nos Papas.* New York: Simon and Schuster, Inc., 1954. Illustrations and sentences describing various occupations. A useful reference for the teacher.

Gessler, Elizabeth, *Guignol à l'école.* New York: Gessler Publishing Co., 1949. A collection of ten plays and directions for making puppets and for constructing a puppet theatre. Suitable for upper elementary and secondary students.

————, *Mon Livre.* New York: Gessler Publishing Co., 1956. Book of short, dramatic scenes, songs and verse useful for special programs. Written for elementary pupils but applicable to beginners on any grade level.

Glasgow, Mary, *Bonjour.* Ontario: Mary Glasgow & Baker Ltd. A small newspaper for pupils of seventh and eighth grades, containing photographs, comics, conversations, crossword puzzles, drawings illustrating simple sentences, and a vocabulary. A seven-inch disc is available for any number.

Instructo Visual Aid Materials. Harrisburg, Pa.: Roberts and Meck, Inc. A packet of 9 x 12 felt pieces in various colors.

Jagendorf, Moritz, *The First Book of Puppets.* New York: Franklin Watts, Inc., 1952. A well-illustrated book that would be useful to any teacher wishing to make and use puppets. It is an introduction to puppetry, with simple directions for making and working various kinds of puppets. The book also contains a few puppet plays in English and directions for clothing the actors, making a stage, creating scenery, and producing a puppet show.

Maps of France, Spain, the Americas, etc. Chicago: Denoyer-Geppert Company; Lincolnwood, Ill.: Banks Upshaw Division, National Textbook Corp. Maps and posters are also available from the French Government Tourist Office, New York, N.Y.

Michel, André, *Tableaux de vocabulaire.* Paris: Fernand Nathan. A set of twelve 32 x 24 charts, most of which provide excellent material for discussion on the elementary or junior high school level.

Mickelson, Lamora. *Action dans la salle de classe*. Cambridge, Mass.: Educators Publishing Service, 1960. Contains plays, poems, fables, and songs. Pen and ink illustrations.

Modern Language Association of America, *Drawings to Accompany French Guides*. Darien, Conn.: Educational Publishing Corp. Eight pictures (Eiffel Tower, outdoor restaurant, street scene, store, schoolroom, bedroom, park and garden, customs inspection) useful for learning of vocabulary. Twenty 8½ x 11 copies of one picture per packet.

Publications on French folk dances, songs, and costumes. Palo Alto, Cal.: French Folklore Society.

Sister Georgiana, *French Dramatizations*. Portland, Me.: J. Weston Walch, Publisher, 1961. Useful in teaching Grades 5 to 10.

Tamin, Marion and George T. Eddington, *Teacher's Guide to Let's Learn French*. New York: Frederick Ungar Publishing Company, 1959. A handbook containing many good ideas for using French in discussing jet planes, scouting, pets, the farm, time, using the telephone, and other subjects of interest to young students.

Taylor, Alice, *France Around the World Program*. New York: Doubleday & Company, Inc., 1956. Includes twenty-five 2 x 3½ color plates to be pasted on the appropriate pages. May be used in sixth grade or junior high school.

ADDRESSES OF INTEREST TO THE TEACHER

Some sources of information for teachers desiring to travel and study in the country whose language they teach:

> Graduate Study
> Institute of International Education
> 1 East 67th Street
> New York 21, New York

For grants and fellowships, study abroad, and UNESCO publications:

> Teacher Exchange
> U.S. Department of Health, Education, and Welfare
> Office of Education
> Educational Exchange and Training Branch
> Teacher Exchange Section
> Washington 25, D.C.

For a summer with a family or, as a group leader with the Experiment in International Living:

> Experiment in International Living
> Putney, Vermont

For information about twin cities:
> Director
> Town Affiliations
> American Municipal Association
> 1612 K Street, N.W.
> Washington 6, D.C.

Sources of information about pupil correspondence:
> Student Letter Exchange
> Waseca, Minnesota

For information about the procuring of pen pals:
> Director
> Bureau de Correspondance Scolaire
> College of Wooster
> Wooster, Ohio

For films, slides, soundtapes, records, filmstrips and exhibits:
> Society for French American Cultural Services and Education Aid
>   (FACSEA)
> 972 Fifth Avenue
> New York 21, N. Y.

The lending library of audio-visual materials of FACSEA is open to all schools and educational organizations. These materials are available on loan for small subscription fee. The catalogue is published every two years.

A good reference library for foreign language teachers:
> Modern Language Materials Center
> 4 Washington Place
> New York 3, N. Y.

This center forms part of the new central offices of the MLA. It provides a reference library of textbooks, films, tapes, discs, maps, and other teaching aids for the use of language teachers in the Northeast and of teachers passing through New York. Glen Wilbern is the Director of the Center, which will continue to evaluate new teaching materials and will publish periodic revisions of the *Selective List of Materials*.

For members of the National Education Association:
> The Department of Foreign Languages of the National Education Association.
> 1201 16th St., N. W.
> Washington 6, D. C.

A new organization devoted to the cause of all foreign languages at all levels. Various publications and services for members.

Index